Healing the Human Mind

Hearing the Guru's teachings,
my mind is struck by His Arrows of Light

Arrows of Light

Healing the Human Mind

Selected Talks

Volume I

His Holiness Baba Virsa Singh

Sterling Paperbacks

STERLING PAPERBACKS
An imprint of
Sterling Publishers (P) Ltd.
A-59, Okhla Industrial Area, Phase-II,
New Delhi-110020.
Tel: 26387070, 26386209; Fax: 91-11-26383788
E-mail: mail@sterlingpublishers.com
www.sterlingpublishers.com

Arrows of Light, Vol I: Healing the Human Mind

ISBN 978 81 207 4468 4

For more information on Babaji's teachings and ongoing programs visit us at www.gobindsadan.org

Photo credits:
Cover Photo: Sergey Bermeniev
All other photos are property of the Trust and Gobind Sadan's archives courtesy of Mary Pat Fisher, except where noted.

Printed and Published by Sterling Publishers Pvt. Ltd.,
New Delhi-110 020.

Contents

Preface

His Holiness Baba Virsa Singh ji left His physical body on Christmas Eve, 24 December 2007. Before leaving, he gave us these arrows to cut through the darkness and spread light throughout the world. We are confident that despite the current state of affairs, the Light will soon dawn. The turmoil we see is only temporary, and darkness is just a backdrop against which the Light can play. The darker it becomes, the more visible the Light will be and the more people will yearn to see it and be drawn to it.

We are witnessing the finale of a period that, despite the technological advances and material glitter, will long be remembered as the Age of Darkness. But in the midst of this darkness and perhaps because of it a great Light descended to earth. He was known to many as Maharaj ji ("The Great King"), to others as Babaji (a respected elder), but His Holiness Baba Virsa Singh ji was only concerned that God's Holy Name and God's praises be sung.

He rekindled the flame of God's love in the hearts of everyone who had the privilege of entering his divine presence, and even in those who just heard his name, much as he re-consecrated the sacred fire that burns continuously at Gobind Sadan, his spiritual community on the outskirts of New Delhi.

He more than anyone else on earth embodied the teachings of Guru Granth Sahib, before which he bowed reverently each day and over which he waved the Chauri Sahib in deep respect: "Love God, work hard, earn an honest living, and share with those in need." And more than anyone else on earth at this time, he stood to defend all religions and the rights of the downtrodden.

He was a truly enlightened being, who by definition is one who sees no divisions among religions, who sees all prophets as One, who sees the image and the presence of the One Eternal God everywhere and in everything, from the tiniest particle to the spectacular stars of the cosmos, and who taught all those who gathered around him to love the Creator in everyone and in all creation. He was a champion of religious pluralism and steadfastly worked to alleviate poverty and terrorism in the world.

May his arrows fly far. May they bring light and joy to your minds and to a troubled world so that the long awaited promise of peace will soon be upon us.

Introduction

Babaji and His Work

Baba Virsa Singh ji is a holy person of Biblical proportions who passed out of his physical body on 24 December, 2007, but is still very present with us. His powerful spirituality was first recognized when he was a child. Born on 20 February, 1934 in the rural village of Raja Jung outside of Lahore, he was uprooted in 1947 by Partition and moved with his family to Sarawan Bodla, a mud-brick village in Punjab, India. He spent his days plowing and working on the family farm, until one day in his late teens he experienced great anguish while cutting fodder for the animals. As the sap poured out, Babaji was consumed with the feeling that he had committed a great sin and prayed to be released from that duty. At once, sores appeared on the soles of his feet, so painful that he could not work. From that time, he began meditating day and night under the Beri tree in the courtyard, calling out to the One whose presence he could feel, "Please come – please show yourself." Babaji became so thin that his father took him to a local doctor. He always laughed when he remembered that time, as the doctor could not find anything wrong with him.

Then one day, an awesome figure appeared to him. It was Baba Siri Chand ji, the great sixteenth-century mystic and elder son of Guru Nanak Dev ji, the first Sikh Guru. Not long thereafter, Baba Siri Chand ji returned and said, "I've brought my Father." There before the young man stood Guru Nanak Dev ji. Babaji recalled the scene vividly: "How can I ever forget the day when He came and stood before me? Baba Siri Chand said, 'I'll introduce you to my Father.' They were both very tall - over 6 feet. Guru Nanak Dev ji wore wooden sandals with a central toe knob and his long gown was mouse-colored. He stood in front of me. Baba Siri Chand ji, said 'My Father has come.' Guru Nanak spoke, 'So you think you need a Guru?' I said 'Yes.' 'Can you see my body?' I said, 'Yes'. 'Can you see my face?' I said 'Yes.' 'Do you see my lips moving? Repeat what I'm about to tell you and share it with others.' Then He said, 'Repeat after me – Ek Onkar Satnam Siri WaheGuru - recite this.' He gave me this shabad (sacred words) and said: 'Give this shabad to the people.' Then he said a very special thing: 'I received Nam this way myself.' That is a very profound thought. Then Guru Gobind Singh ji came. He had His own ways. He gave me many boons."

After that, Baba Siri Chand ji and Guru Gobind Singh ji were constantly with him, instructing the young man in strict meditation and in service to humanity. It was then that Baba Virsa Singh was shown that he would have to work very hard, that his fame and wealth would spread, that he would develop great farms, and perhaps most strange, that he would have a great following in Russia. When the boy began healing intractable diseases by giving people leaves from the Beri tree where he sat - or when the leaves were gone, simply by dipping his fingers in water - bringing the dead back to life, and transforming people's lives, villagers recognized that great spiritual powers were developing within him. They began to gather around him, and all have stories of the miracles that happened daily among his followers.

Obeying the command of God, Babaji moved from place to place, from Karnal in Haryana, North of Bareilly in UP, to Shimla, Amritsar, Chandigarh and finally Delhi, reminding people of dharma, the Eternal Truth of all religions beyond any sectarian divisions. He was directed to some dry, thorny, rocky land at the south end of Delhi offered by a devotee, Sardarni Nirlep Kaur, a prominent Sikh leader. And in June of 1968 he began to develop that land into what is now Gobind Sadan, "God's House Without Walls" – a paradise of peaceful gardens, tree-lined paths, round-the-clock devotional centers, and a free community kitchen for people of all faiths and all social levels where miracles are everyday occurrences. He developed farms elsewhere as well, including the huge model farm known as Shiv Sadan, reclaimed from a dangerous flood-prone wasteland on the banks of the holy river Ganges.

People of all faiths and many countries came to Babaji at Gobind Sadan for his blessings and guidance, for practical spiritual training, for devotional worship, and for seva (voluntary service). Those working on the farms do strenuous manual labor from dawn to dusk, raising lush productive crops with yields far exceeding those in surrounding areas. The sevadars do not tire; they say they feel invigorated and blessed by the work. As they work, Babaji had encouraged them to silently recite God's Holy Name in loving remembrance ("Ek Onkar Sat Nam Siri Wahe Guru"—" There is One God whose name is Truth, Praise the Ever Greater, ever more wondrous God").

The work on the farms supports Babaji¡'s mission to overcome poverty and religious conflict and bring peace to both individuals and the world. To heal the sick and poor in spirit, prayers are offered around the clock. To uplift the deserving poor, langars (free community meals where people of all castes sit side by side on the ground), medical care, and schooling for children are offered free of cost. And to teach reverence for all those who bring God's message and their teachings, according to Babaji's inspiration there are frequent interfaith gatherings and celebrations of the major holidays of all religions.

Baba Virsa Singh made no claim to being a guru; he did not seek fame, followers, or money. He said, "I am just trying to be a better human being. What I say is not new. I just repeat the commands of God so that people will remember them." The lives and teachings of the Sikh Gurus are the model for his practical work, yet he continually referred to the timeless teachings revealed by all prophets. He stressed that sectarian divisions have been created by humans, not by God or God's Messengers. His basic program is the same for everyone: Recite Nam, read *Jaap Sahib* (Guru Gobind Singh's empowering hymn of God's praises), do seva and rise early in the morning to thank God and in meditation, look within yourself to battle with your own evils.

Babaji was highly respected as a world class leader, by scholars (though he had not received any formal worldly education), by government officials (though he sought no one's favor), by scientists (who find truth in Babaji's words and presence even if they have been religious skeptics), and by religious leaders and devotees of all faiths (for he sincerely loved and encouraged appreciation of all Prophets and scriptures). Although multitudes have been blessed, healed and personally transformed through his influence and by following the practical program he recommended, Babaji continually said, "God is the only Doer, the One who gives you everything. Give all your love to God."

I

Controlling The Human Mind

When a river overflows its banks it does great damage to the surrounding areas.

But when a person's mind is not controlled, he can destroy entire countries.

Happiness

Ego is the greatest disease that plagues humanity today. It grows out of our ignorance. To obtain enlightenment, we must recite Nam, God's Holy Name. As the Gurus taught, Kalyug (Age of Darkness) has come, sow the seed of Nam (God's Holy Name). In order to find happiness and contentment in Kalyug we must recite Nam.

When we take birth in this world, our lives are affected by what we have done in our previous lives. We must understand that the life of the spirit is very long. When we say someone has died, their body has died but their spirit and the gyan that dwelt within them never dies. The Power within the body never dies. That's why when we leave this body we take birth again.

We receive our births according to our previous deeds. Whatever we do all day long forms our sanskar (fate) and wherever we take birth our fate goes with us. That's why Guru Sahib says: "Our mind is blackened with the filth of many lives." What dirt is the Guru speaking of? The wrongs we have done in our past lives. Guru Nanak says: "When our body and clothes get dirty we wash them with soap. But how do we wash the filth from our minds? With Nam."

When we recite Nam, the effect of our past deeds are changed. This power does not come from outside us. It is within. When we recite Nam and do good deeds it becomes manifest and we'll be able to feel it. The best deed we can do is reciting Nam. When we recite Nam all the goodness within us will become very powerful and the negativity will decrease.

Then we will never judge another's bad actions because we will be too busy reviewing our own bad habits. When will we be able to judge ourselves? When we approach Truth. Which Truth am I speaking of? The Truth that lies within. God's power which dwells within us. God never comes nor goes. He is Eternal and

His power lies within everyone. When we recite Nam we can feel His power.

When we feel His Power a great change occurs within us. Now we are constantly saying, "What will happen to my job, my children, my house, and what will happen to us?" But when we recite Nam, then we realize that God knows what will happen to us and our family. These are just our desires.

Dharam, God's eternal law, teaches us to keep doing good deeds and don't look for the results. Keep loving God but if you are waiting for the results it's not true love. Maharaj ji says, just look to His love and then our worries will go away. We'll realize, "God created life in the water and provides for all those creatures." There are no shops there. When God gives you birth He is so concerned about you that He provides for you too.

What should we worry about? Never doing anything to hurt someone else's feelings. Even hurting someone's feelings will earn us bad luck. Whenever a thought even crosses our minds, becomes our karmas. But how can we change our thoughts? By studying that subject which teaches us.

Dharam is also a school about which Guru Nanak said: "To study this subject I had to practice tapasya (spiritual discipline) for many lives. And then I discovered that God is everywhere" When He saw the extent of nature, the Guru said that God is very powerful. He said there are millions of earths and skies but we can only see one. We see one sun but when the Guru saw God's splendor he saw millions like this one, millions of moons and there was still no end to the cosmos. He said – there are no pillars to hold up the sky – God created the heavens without the need of pillars to support them.

But when did he discover that? When he meditated and when he said that my Guru is everywhere. He is Eternal and he is present in everything. When did he say, "My mind is full of dirt?" When he meditated.

Today we should clearly understand that what we call gurdwaras (Sikh temples), mandirs (Hindu and Jain temples), masjids

(Mosques), churches, temples, or synagogues are all schools to train our minds. There are rules in these schools too. Always tell the truth. Never lie. When we enter this school we will be taught, "from today on we have to tell the truth." Then Guru ji said that we should never steal and we shouldn't hurt anyone's feelings, nor deny anyone's rights. What should we be concerned about? We should always be concerned about another's well-being and happiness – our neighbors, our city, our country and then we will be worried that everybody should love God and all of His creation. We should never hate anyone.

But what do we do now? We go to religious places and we put forth our worldly demands. What does this school teach us? We should ask God for Nam because nothing else will stay for ever.

"Oh God please give me your Nam and all the hunger of my mind will go away." Maharaj ji tells us how we should act when we go to a place of worship. But we think that just by going to gurdwara we'll be blessed. There is no school or college in the world where you can get a degree simply by going there. There is no place of learning where you can change or improve yourself just by entering the gates.

Right now our biggest weakness is that we go to God's school simply as part of our routine and keep looking at our watch. We go and bow our heads but our mind is not there even for even two minutes. Then we leave and spend the rest of our time in our offices

We should realize why we aren't happy today

Happiness doesn't come from big houses, big positions, nor from money. Maharaj ji says even a sinner can amass wealth. We can acquire worldly things by cheating, but happiness can not be bought.

Wherever we recite Nam we will be happy, and we will be fearless. Fearlessness does not mean that we will be the aggressor and kill or hurt someone or deny their rights. Fearlessness means that if someone is being oppressed or someone's rights or religion is being denied or someone is hurting another, you defend them. Someone who loves God – a truly religious person – shouldn't care whether the victim is rich or poor, he should help that person because they are a human being and because they are oppressed. So one who is fearless will stand and say "Don't oppress that person" That is what we mean by "chint parai," to worry about others. The Guru said:

"The world is burning – from whatever door they approach you please bless them. God these people have big houses and big positions but they have forgotten You – they have forgotten Your power. They lacked wisdom but their ignorance was great." Then Maharaj ji said, "Come wake up and love that God who is fearless and has no enmity because the one who loves God has no enemy and no fear of any body. Why? Because he is under God's protection. Maharaj ji said: "When you pray to the Fearless One all your fears go away."

Why is there fear within us? Because we are not enlightened. But when we recite Nam we will become like Him. Guru Gobind Singh ji says:

"Human beings are like the ocean. A wave arises from the ocean and recedes into the water again."

Similarly human beings are part of God. Everybody has God within them. Everybody has gyan within. Everyone has God's power within them. Everyone has fearlessness. But it doesn't show. We say that God is everywhere. God is always with us, and if He is always within us Guru Sahib is telling us that fearlessness is also within us. So where does the fear come from. Why are you afraid?

What is fear? It is our selfishness, our past karma, our ego and ignorance. So let us recognize that our places of worship are not just for ritual, but schools to train our minds. Maharaj ji said serving your Guru is the most difficult task but it is also an ocean of happiness. This is a school where we learn to be good human beings. Right now we are not even good human beings. We deny people's rights, we hurt other's feelings, we back bite, we don't act justly. Human beings should not do these things. This is all our ignorance. But the One who is enlightened won't do any of these things and when he sees someone's bad points he will immediately look within himself and see his own weaknesses. That is enlightened thinking.

He understands that if this other person made this mistake I can make it too. If we look at the story from the life of the Lord Jesus:

Jesus was walking when he saw people stoning a woman. He stopped and asked why they were hurting her. They said she had committed a sin. So Jesus replied, "First look within yourself. If any of you have not sinned then stone her. If not don't hurt her." When they took a minute to think, they started to see their own mistakes and forgot the mistake she had made. Then nobody had the courage to stone her. They all dropped their stones. Why? When they heard the teachings of religion they all went within themselves and found their own faults. Right now we should try to develop that power which is hidden within us. We should try to feel that power within us.

The power to remain happy, the power to act justly and the power to speak the truth is within us. But why don't we realize this? Because we never even spend ten or fifteen minutes on this subject and still we say, 'I spent ten minutes and I can't concentrate.' We can't just spend ten minutes and expect results. The mind is always running. It's been running wild for a long time. How can we bring it back in ten minutes.

If you let your horse run wild all day you can't expect to tame it and turn it for home quickly.

The more we meditate the more we will become calm and happy in our homes, and our offices, because we have accepted this course of happiness. What is this subject of Happiness – Dharam – God's eternal laws.

What is dharam? When you follow the rules and law of religion. What is law and order? We don't have to go to a building to take training. We have to understand the teachings and when we go home we have to follow them. We have to act justly in society and in our offices. We don't have to sit in one room. When we mediate the special power inside us will burst forth. When it bursts forth we will feel such a pull from God within us that it will never go away. That force is so strong that even if someone cuts your head off it will still be there – if someone is cut to shreds the power is still there. That's why we say the Power of God never dies. It will always be there.

We have to feel that power. How can we live forever? Who can live forever? Those who have attained enlightenment. How do you become enlightened, through meditation, by reciting Nam. Now we are worried that we will all die someday. Forget about death. Humans don't die. It's like moving to a new house or being transferred to a new department in your company.

First of all if we recite Nam this fear will go away. The life of the spirit is very long. As long as humans have existed that human spirit has been present. The Power of God, the Light of God which is within them never dies.

Guru Gobind Singh ji said: "Throughout all creation there is just one Light, we can never increase or diminish it."

If we recite Nam we will feel that Light the Kabir Sahib described: "Ram and Kabir have become one. When I recited Nam I heard God saying Dhan Kabir (how great is Kabir) and I was praising Ram, Ram, Ram"

What is Ram – that which is omnipresent and eternal. It is Ram who stays alive. Ram who give us income, Ram who gives us life, and who is within everything. Kabir said to Ram, "I am saying Ram, Ram why are you saying Kabir, Kabir? So Ram answered, "Ram and Kabir have become one and nobody can tell us apart. Because you have recognized that Power at this time your gyan – enlightenment - is no different. Your mind has become like the water in the Ganges and Hari and Ram are behind you saying Kabir, Kabir."

"How did the mind become so pure when I said those two words Ram, Ram – and enlightenment manifested?" I said, "The world is scared of death and I will be happy when I die because it is only when you die that you meet this Power. What is death? You leave this body you die and become one with that Power that Light – with the power of enlightenment."

That's why never forget that if we think by taking flowers to God's home, He will be satisfied, or that God will be happy by our contributing money in His temples, that is pure ignorance and in this state of ignorance our lives are over and we take birth again. So let us rid ourselves of this misconception. God's love has no connection with flowers or money. It doesn't depend on our worldly position. The only relationship we can have with God is through love.

At the time of Lord Krishna, there was a very rich man and he thought he had a lot of power and could control everything. He invited Lord Krishna to his home for a feast. Lord Krishna told him, "Oh King, who could come to your home? I like the poor Bidar who loves me. He doesn't have a big house but we spent the whole night talking about our Beloved and forgot to eat, forgot to sleep and we were singing His praises until morning." Maharaj ji says: "Gobind craves the devotion of those who love Him." God doesn't want our money or our flowers or care whether we use marble in the temples we build. Nor is God happy if we bow before Him. He is pleased by our love. Why? This is the basic teaching of all religions. It is the law of Dharam: to love God. We may be happy building marble temples but that has nothing to do with God. It has no connection with love.

God helps the poor and takes away our weaknesses. He takes away our bad habits. The greatest weakness he removes is our ego. "I opened a big factory, I made a big home. That is ego. Maharaj ji says, "Ego and Nam can not exist together." So as Guru Gobind Singh ji taught us: even my family is not mine. It is all yours. But when do we gain enlightenment. When we meditate and recite Nam. Every time Guru Gobind Singh ji tied his turban, he would say, "Tav Parshad," this is all your blessings. When he mounted his horse or even whenever he ate, "Lord, It's all Your blessings." So when we recite Nam we will learn to say: "It's all your blessings."

When we get in our car, when buy a big house, we will say, "It's your blessings. I am not worthy of this". "I am very good, I deserve all of this. I have a very good mind." Then Ego arises and the Ego wants to stay in the same place with Nam. But they can not live together. You can visit gurdwara or mandir everyday and rub your noses on the ground, but God won't accept you in His house. Love God and think everyone is good. Don't judge anybody and you will change and you will be blessed.

But now when we go to the mandir and gurdwara the only thing we gain is more ego. We give money to those singing God's praises (kirtan). Prayer and kirtan have no connection with money. The only connection there is love.

Right now we go to gurdwara and mandir donate money and come home. We ourselves break the rules of the gurdwara. Guru Nanak Dev ji said, "The law of the gurdwara is 'work hard for your living, and out of those earnings, help those in need." Who are the needy? Those who can't afford food, or the tuition to educate their children. Maharaj ji says we should pay that child's tuition. If they can't afford clothes, buy them clothes and food.

Someone once asked Maharaj ji, "If on the way to Gurdwara we have money and we meet some poor people who need food or clothes or medicine what should we do?" Maharaj ji replied, "When you help those in need your donation reaches me."

But what do we do? We think the Guru will be happy when we bring money to the Gurdwara. But the Guru doesn't want the money. The Guru's program is love, faith and truth. But we want our ego.

So from now on when we go to our places of worship let us try to follow the teachings, and not just bow our heads. When we return home, let us put them into practice. If someone continues making the same mistakes or committing the same sins after going to gurdwara, it shows it has had no effect on him. Wherever a true gurdwara is and a true devotee, there should be justice, love, faith and truth. For these are the teachings of that institution.

Maharaj ji says: "When the whole world is yours, how can we say who is good and who is bad. O Lord, please bless them all"

But we are like clay dolls – puppets dancing all day. When we win we become very proud. We become happy that my thought or plan was very good. But when we lose, we cry. Our minds and plans may be very good, even when we lose, but our ego gets in the way and creates disappointment.

Any person who doesn't meditate will not have kindness in their minds, and if he is not kind, he will not act justly. Remember, one day we all will leave our bodies. There are no two thoughts about that. And when we leave – our spirit will be tormented. We are worried, "What will happen now, what will happen now?" Our spirit will keep saying the same thing and when we take birth again we won't have any peace. We will be forever nervous. So that is why we should recite Nam.

Whoever recites Nam is forever happy. Our Guru will give us happiness here and in His kingdom.

When I speak of the Guru, I mean the one which sits within us both. He is within everyone. But the difference is that we have different subjects. Mine is the subject of enlightenment. If you don't meditate and follow the rules you will never become enlightened.

So today we should all decide that we want to stay happy. Money can't make us happy, neither can big houses or cars or factories. The more material things we gain the more worried we become. The only way we can stay happy is to meditate, recite Nam.

When we recite Nam, the Guru will take away our bad habits. Who is Guru? The shabad, Nam, that which brings Light. If you ask what that Light is, it is beyond description. Guru Nanak Dev ji was able to describe it.

Lord Krishna told Arjun – "It's your duty, it's your dharam to pick up your weapon. But Arjun said "All my family and my Guru are standing on the other side" Krishna replied, "Who is the guru of your soul? Gyan is the soul's guru. Weapons can't kill that gyan. Gyan lives forever." So Krishan Maharaj ji said "Gyan is your Guru"

When we get up in the morning we recite Nam and meditate. What do I mean by meditation? To love God and recite Nam. Nam is the Guru. The body is not the Guru. This body will not be here forever. It will die but Nam will never leave. "My Guru is eternal. He is the one who brings light to all creation and He resides in everything"

That Guru has no shape, nor color, has no body: "Wahe Guru," the Guru who is beyond all description. He was speaking of Nam not a body. And when we recite Nam we will understand that we have a Guru. Just by bowing, we don't have a Guru. Only when we obey his hukam (divine order) can we say we have a Guru. Hukam doesn't mean leaving our home or work or leaving your family. Maharaj ji teaches us to recite Nam even while staying with our families, our factories, our home, or work. Right now, we think we have made all these things and forget that it is God who gave us everything.

We have a duty to work. Our duty is to do His job and thank Him. Thank Him for the energy to work all day and then thank Him for our sleep at night. God takes care of us even at night. Your body is functioning, your heart is beating. We have His energy.

When we wake up in the morning we should thank Him for the good night's sleep and the strength to work. And if we thank Him, the force of Truth within will be so powerful that we will always be happy.

Right now we are unhappy. We are always worrying "what will happen?" We don't have faith. The One who has given us our body will take care of us; He is worried about us. He doesn't look at our faults. He is always forgiving us. But we will only know this when we approach that Power within.

We don't even spend ten minutes in meditation and yet we claim there is no God. We won't go near that power. We aren't even willing to spend ten minutes yet we still claim that God doesn't exist. That's not our subject to declare whether God exists or not. Kabir spent thirty-six years in mediation. He did 3 twelve-year courses in mediation. And we have no idea how many courses he completed in his past lives. But only after thirty-six years did he say that "My mind has accepted that God exists." What is God. He is everywhere. God is Truth. God is fearlessness, God is love, God is faith. Kabir Sahib said "Today my mind has realized that God exists," but that was only after thirty-six years of mediation. Kabir Sahib said, "Now I say there is a God, but people don't believe me. They ask where He is. It took me thirty-six years to realize that He is sitting inside you. He is everywhere. It took me thirty-six years of searching and then only after I went within and forgot about myself.

So that is why unless we recite Nam or meditate we can't say He is fearless, we can't say how great His power is. This is also a course. Just think today you are sitting in God's school – the School of Dharam, and from today on if we meditate and say He is fearless, we will become fearless. When we say, He is Truth we will speak truth. When we say He is Just, He will give us the strength to act justly. We will say He is the source of all happiness and we will become happy. Then we will say He is Joy and we will be filled with Joy. When will this happen? Only when we meditate.

Meditation is the course of Happiness

If we don't want to meditate, recite Nam or offer prayers we won't gain true happiness. But even if we offer prayers and don't set aside our worldly desires, God won't accept our prayers. Only those prayers are acceptable that are full of love. Wherever there is self-interest there is no love. And where there is no love there is no enlightenment. Where there is no enlightenment there will never be light. This is why we go to holy places: to ask God to give us that which remains forever. Whatever material gift we ask from God only brings more troubles with it. Let us learn to ask for that Nam. With Nam all our desires will go away and we will be happy.

Always remember that a Gurdwara is also a school. There is no school which doesn't provide training. But we are like students who go to university with books in hand, walk around the campus once, and leave. If you ask the professor if he knows us, he'll say, "No." Just by taking a trip to the university you won't get a degree. Similarly, you can't expect to gain enlightenment just by going to a place of worship without following the rules. The only thing you'll receive is a false sense of satisfaction that God may have forgiven you. But that's only your imagination and it's false. We are not forgiven just by bowing. Maharaj ji says, "What's the point in bowing when you don't follow the Guru's orders?"

If only by bowing you think you will get blessings, look at the hunter who lies in wait for many hours. He has no connection with God. So let us understand what it really means to bow: recognize our mistakes and seek God's help to correct them. We should ask, Maharaj ji what is the hukam for me? The essence of all our worship is to seek God's forgiveness for the mistakes of our past and seek His guidance to follow a path of goodness in the future.

No religion will allow you to ask forgiveness then go out and commit the same mistake again and again. All teach that we should seek forgiveness that we never make those mistakes again, and we are able to put them behind us.

Hollow Worship

But we have turned our time in worship into an empty ritual. That is why there is no difference between those who go to places of worship and those who don't. Those who spend time in worship come home and still may lie and cheat. So the others say, "What's the use of going, what's there for me?" They are both the same, there's no difference. The one who goes says that God will fulfill my wishes and the other goes to a worldly power to get help. Neither has any connection to God. Where God is concerned, there is love. Where there is love there is sacrifice and wherever there is sacrifice there is faith.

So from today on we have to decide whether we want to stay happy or be worried. Now we are worried all day long. But Maharaj ji instructs us to keep working and not to look for the results. The only desire we should have is: "Oh God make me the way you want me to be. Have me do those things which are pleasing to You." We should have a desire to thank God all day long and love Him and then we will be eternally happy.

The Battle over the Human Mind

To the owner of a major public relations firm

It is our thoughts which create the divisions that turn us against each other. So let us remember there is only one God – one Truth – one path which we can all walk together. The God I'm speaking of is omnipresent but it's only when we meditate on Him that God becomes visible, and appears to us from within all Creation.

When we turn our thoughts towards Him, His light comes within us and we are able to see God within ourselves. And when we see God within we will definitely say: "God you are everywhere within everything – in the water, in the earth – you are omnipresent." "And if you exist in everyone then how can I be angry with anyone."

With whom am I to be angry?

Think about it, if God is within everyone who am I to be angry with? Who should I attack – whose rights should I deny? And once we understand that God is within everyone then Truth will emerge – peace will emerge.

What is Christianity, what is Islam, what is a Hindu what is a Parsee? These names are all manmade. They have nothing to do with God.

When we see that there is one God who exists everywhere then we begin to question where did these boundaries come from?

They've come from our thoughts – and we've created our own names. And by using these separate names we create anger.

We've forgotten the One we pray to

The slogan that is heard coming from these boundaries is: "My religion is the best." This song is being sung everywhere. Everyone is singing the same song. But dharam is not present. Religion has become a matter of rules and regulations – how to pray. The method has taken over – but we've forgotten the One whom we pray to. All we have to do is remember God, turn our minds to God and that becomes our prayer. It is simply a matter of directing our minds, our thoughts. But we're busy telling people how they should hold their hands.

We are just preaching to them. God dwells within us, but unless and until we understand that God is within us order will never come in society. Disorder and disruption will remain at all levels. Because whenever there's unrest, it starts with our minds. And what I mean by "mind" is our thoughts.

Conquer your mind and you will rule the world

The body has nothing to do with it. The body simply responds to our thoughts. We move according to where our thoughts direct us. So the greatest issue is how to control our minds. Guru Nanak said "if we conquer our minds – we conquer the world." If you want to conquer the world first conquer your minds. People are afraid. But what does gyan instruct us? "If the fearless one dwells us within why are you afraid?"

God has no enmity with anyone; then where do those qualities come from? If He's within you how can these things arise? Where does the anger come from? Where does revenge come from? So conquer your mind and you will rule the world.

The mind creates the thought to commit a crime, corruption, or deny people's rights. So everything boils down to this small point – how can we conquer the mind? Until we can control the mind, forget that peace will ever come.

The arrows of the mind are very sharp

They won't let good thoughts arise. Sometimes our adversaries will speak with great anger. They will deny someone's rights, attack someone's character – their minds fire those arrows twenty-four hours a day. The only way to stop their attack is to control our minds.

So don't get angry at them. They have no control over their thoughts.

Even when we try to explain our position they can't understand. Their arrows are so sharp they don't let us near them. But once they throw down their weapons, they'll start talking about peace. So my focus from the very beginning has been to teach people how to bring our minds under control.

Clash between our auras

Everyone has an aura. Some are good and some are bad. Our aura comes from our thoughts - the worse your thoughts are, the worse your aura becomes. If your thoughts are pure, your aura will reflect the purity. The clash today is between the auras, between the aura of anger and the aura of love.

It may take some time but eventually the aura of love will defeat the aura of anger. Then the arrows of anger will fall. In the meantime, those with anger will definitely attack you. So strengthen your minds and look to God.

Tear down the boundaries

Because peace won't come until we are able to tear down the boundaries. So let us focus on ways to break these walls down. But this will require gyan, a lot of time counseling the people, and linking them to God. Because after all the power for peace is with Him. So let's take the power from God with which we can break the arrows of evil. Then God will give you His blessings and you will definitely win.

The battle is raging

When the blessings come, you must rise up like a lion and break those evil arrows. This is a very vicious war. Even though you can't see it, the battle is raging at full force. We must finish this battle. I've been fighting all my life; taking God's power and speaking. But I'm very happy.

God will never say that He's not involved in the battle. Because He is behind this battle. Guru Gobind Singh ji said: "I've seen

You appear in battles – You are the one who creates the conflict – but You also bring peace. You first create the conflicts – and then you settle the disputes." As long as there is life God is always present. When God's light leaves then we can't say a person is at fault. God won't speak after we're dead. So ask God now to bless them: "take away their arrows and break them because they are under Your control." But keep fighting. These bad arrows can only be broken by gyan. The arrows of evil are weak and gyan is very powerful. But we must do the fighting. It's a battle of thoughts, of opinions, through dialogue. Truth will always prevail, so start the battle. Strengthen your thoughts, purify your thoughts, and cleanse your minds. Drive out the bad thoughts.

Make a firm commitment and be determined that you will win. Guru Gobind Singh ji said: "I have full faith that I'll definitely win – because my enemies don't have any goal behind their arrows. They only want to upset people – deny people's rights – make people suffer. My arrows' goal is to free the people. God will always help me and I'll definitely win. So keep fighting and you too will surely win.

From time immemorial, whenever evil has spread through the world, a force for peace has taken birth. Then some others arise who want to share the message and become partners in the mission. And to strengthen the message they join him. Slowly they come together.

It's a matter of quality. The majority has never accomplished any great works. So stress quality and leave the majority to their own devices. Ignore what the majority is doing.

Just go slowly. I've made my goal. I've been walking on the path. Keep waiting for the day that your goal and your feelings will defeat the other forces.

Those who have no Truth are like trees without roots

Those who have no Truth are like a tree standing on the banks of a river – it has no base – no roots. All the river has to do is rise up and it will wash the tree away.

If you build a sand castle – it's always in danger. When a storm comes up, the rain will wash it away. So wherever Truth does not exist – that person is like a house of sand or a tree without roots. They have no foundation.

Catch the public's ear

When this idea catches the ear of the public, they'll become alert. Right now the message that reaches them is not in their control. Why are governments corrupt? Why is corruption present in society? Because people have been misled. They think that poison is amrit (nectar). It is definitely poison, but they drink it like it were amrit. This is the way the play has been created.

Peace will definitely come

Peace will definitely come. You don't have to worry, just keep walking this path. I keep talking about this. In my entire life I have never been defeated, either in gyan, in discussion, or by another's opinions. It always takes a little effort to educate people and then they agree that I am right. No matter how high a person's position has been they've always come down. One thing you must commit to before you walk on this path, is to always control your anger.

Smile when people attack you

People will be very angry with you. They're very hardened and they will attack you. But just smile at them, and that smile will calm their anger. If you get angry in return then they've won, their mission is successful. They've made you angry. They've achieved their goal and we've failed in ours. No matter what they say or do, if you smile, laugh, and welcome them they've lost. Just keep forging ahead, everything will be all right.

They themselves are unhappy

Remember all those who've created these boundaries are unhappy themselves. But they've taken such a strong position that it is hard for them to retreat. They've moved so far in that direction. They've openly stated their positions. But when they begin to regret their actions and retract their statements then everything will normalize. So don't worry, they will regret their policies.

Many very angry people have come to me, but I keep laughing. I keep in mind, "If I get angry then he will win, so I will defeat him by not getting angry." So don't worry because peace will definitely come as peace is a very great power. But it will take some time.

God Himself is thinking

God Himself is thinking. The cries of the world are reaching him. People are not letting God sleep. People's cries are ringing all around him. So He's thinking, and all it takes is for God to think and everything will be all right. In Islam, it is said that in the beginning Allah was alone. And He thought "how can I create the world?" Then He spoke – "*kun*" – "Be" and that sound carried throughout creation. In Gurbani it's written, that God spoke, "*Ek Onkar"(One God)* and the seeds of creation spread throughout the world. God's voice exists in everything.

The storm of gyan is on its way

Now the Voice of Creation, the One who spoke is still present, and when He speaks that sound will penetrate everyone's minds. And gyan will manifest within everyone. Even where gyan doesn't exist, the darkness will disappear when it arrives. The storm of gyan is on its way. So be happy and keep spreading the message. Laugh and accept what's happening. Then God will be happy, you'll be happy, and peace will come.

Arrows of anger – arrows of peace

Remember that people's words are sharper than arrows. But God's power will not let those arrows hurt us. The enemy only stops when he has fired all his arrows and you are still standing there laughing. If you get angry then they've won. Their arrows are tipped with anger. And your arrows are tipped with peace. And peace can never get angry – peace can never be disappointed. Peace is just filled with happiness, so no matter what someone does, it can't disturb that happiness. So that's why I tell you that all my life, from my very childhood, I've watched this battle and just kept moving ahead.

The sign of peace

Because it's their mission to put obstacles in your path and try to block your way. And it's your mission to keep moving towards your goal. I'm not going to listen to one side or the other. I'm going to achieve my goal. Keep your eyes closed, your ears closed, and your mouth shut to these distractions, and keep moving along the path. Forge ahead. That is the sign of peace.

Don't listen to your detractors

Don't listen to your detractors. Don't pay any attention to them. Don't respond to them. Just keep moving ahead. Then you'll defeat them. Evil will fall at your feet, and peace will stand and spread its canopy over you. And so there's only one way to bring peace. Be strong and forge ahead.

No better time to speak of Dharam

There has never been a better time to talk about dharam in the world. It may seem strange but everyone is beset by worry, everyone has made mistakes, everyone feels that they have sinned, and everyone is infected by this disease. So when they receive the medicine of peace they'll be cured. They're very sick. They're so infected by their own egos that they have no way out. Even if they receive a little bit of the medicine of peace they'll feel better. So when you begin dispensing peace, they themselves will seek you out. They'll hear that you have the medicine they need.

Cooling the fires of hatred

Guru Nanak described Kali Yug (the Age of Darkness) as very hot and Nam (God's Holy Name) as being the only way to cool it off. So when the power of gyan is so cooling the heat won't last long. Fire can't withstand ice. And Peace is another form of cool ice. Keep your faith and forge ahead. This is a very powerful time and everything will be all right. Many people have tried to fight with me. I've met many who've said there is no God. And I respond, "If God doesn't exist why are you so afraid of Him?" You're clearly afraid of Him otherwise you wouldn't declare God doesn't exist. God is so powerful that you're already worried." Then they're a little shaken and admit that God must be there if "I'm taking His Name." So that's why I say, there is no such thing as an atheist or a believer, it's a matter of gyan.

No one is an atheist

Last year I went to Russia and told them that it's a very small matter: "You've been saying there is no God, now you'll start saying there's One God," and such a great battle will be finished in two minutes. That appealed to them, because they truly want peace. And they agreed with me. They resisted me for a little while and then laid down their weapons. But it all happened with great love. That love has spread over them. And they've developed this longing for God. So that's why I say, after going to Russia, there is no such thing as an atheist.

They just need the light of gyan

Where did the darkness come from? There's a bulb in the room, but it was off. When we walk in and turn it on, suddenly there's light. Similarly a person's light of gyan is turned off. If you turn it on, it will give light. Then you'll ask where the darkness went.

The darkness has disappeared and the bulb that was off has been turned on. People developed a habit of living in darkness. Now they'll see the Light and learn to live in the Light. So it's a great problem, but at the same time, the solution is very simple. Because God is sitting within you. He's smiling and laughing and watching the drama. After all He Himself created the drama. Without the drama He'd be bored. He's happy being part of the drama. Guru Gobind Singh calls God the dance within the dancer. And tells God, you are such a great dancer that you have the whole world dancing. God is very happy. So just keeping working.

My mission is to laugh, show love and share God's power freely

So my mission is to keep laughing, show love to everyone, and take God's power. Keep laughing and take His love, and keep laughing while you share it with others. He doesn't ask anything in return for His love, so don't you ask anything of those you share it with. He gives freely and laughs, so don't you put a price on it either, just laugh and share it. After all love has no price tag. The price of love is love itself. So go calmly, laugh and play. Remember God is watching. It's very good. This is my program, to be happy and share happiness.

Sometimes we argue with God

Sometimes we fight with God – sometimes we complain. But we always love God. One day Nam Dev, the great saint, was very upset and cried out to God: "What's the use of sending a boat after a person has already drowned? I have so much love for you and I want to meet you. If I die and then you send the boat to get me, I won't be able to see the boat." But that was full of love since he was missing God. He knew that God would come to rescue him in a minute.

The boundaries suffocate us

God keeps showering His love on us and we should keep taking it. I know you know He loves you. So break down those boundaries and bring dharam in the world. These boundaries suffocate us.

They drive out our happiness. Our choice is finished. Our taste is finished. But God is pure enjoyment. He's not in a building. He's sitting everywhere, in the mountains, in the trees, in the oceans.

The trees are singing His praises, the ocean is singing his praises, and the flowers share their fragrance. This is their way of calling to God to notice them. And God does look at them and enjoy their beauty. They are all competing for His attention. The air is fanning Him, the flowers are His perfume, the sun and the moon are his lamps, and the stars are a Mandal (palette) of light, and they are all singing His praises. And He's happy. So see Him everywhere, talk with Him everywhere, and be happy wherever you go. It's not a matter of just saying that He is omnipresent.

God is not Stubborn He will share His Peace

So talk with Him, laugh and play with God. Keep loving Him. Peace will definitely come. Peace resides with God and He will definitely give it to us. God is not stubborn. Just knock a little and He'll open His door. And as soon as the door opens, there will be nothing but Light. He's very loving. And when He opens the door, He'll laugh greatly. He won't look at you angrily and say, "Who's that knocking on my door in the middle of the night" So keep laughing, be happy, and everything will be all right.

We're God's guests

If you look at it, we're all God's guests. Look at the beautiful gardens and lawns. He's made lakes and flowers. And He's made everything just for us. What a wonderful Father He is who first makes provisions for all his children's needs. When we are guests of such a great host, how can we be unhappy? That's why I tell you to be happy. We're all guests and let's keep walking His path.

Simple points from illiterate prophets

I keep sharing these simple points. I'm not one to delve into great philosophy. And God is not a philosophy, He's real. When the Angel came to the Prophet Mohammed, he said "Speak," and Mohammed replied, "What should I say?" The angel repeated, "Read this." "I can't read – I'm illiterate. I haven't been to school." God spoke with those who were illiterate. And the well educated and those with degrees were sitting on one side, but God chose to speak to those with no education. God knew that the educated people would ask Him so many questions that they wouldn't let Him speak. So that's why I say that God is not a philosophy. Love God and take love from Him. Every prophet has spoken of love.

Management creates the conflict

Management always creates the conflict. There has always been enmity between management and gyan. It still exists today and it will continue into the future. But keep walking your path because gyan always wins. Gyan will win today and will be victorious in the future. So go peacefully. Laugh and be happy. When we have such a great Father why shouldn't we be happy?

Why Meditation is Essential

Throughout the world, people go to religious places where they bow their heads, pray, and pay their respects in their own ways. Why then doesn't humanity change? To change, it is essential to meditate.

Our mind is a jungle of anger, greed, lust, attachment, and ego. How can this jungle be cleared? The best tool is meditation.

We recite prayers with our tongue, but our mind is not listening. It is wandering, always turning towards the negative. Meditation will unite our mind with the sacred words we are reciting.

When the two unite, our condition will become like that of Kabir, who after continually reciting "Ram, Ram," said, "The mind has become pure like the water of the Ganges. Ram (God) is following me, calling, 'Kabir, Kabir.' Ram and Kabir have become one – no one can distinguish between us."

The Guru said, "Oh mind, you are the manifestation of the Light – recognize your essence." Let us recognize that we and the light are one. Delve into yourself and recognize the Light of God. As the Guru has said, "God kindled the Light within you, thus you took birth in this world." Only after God lit the Light in you did you take birth, start to walk, to talk, to understand, and to develop a mind of your own. With meditation, you will realize that power of God and free yourself of the bad tendencies within you.

Peace for the stressed mind

People do not understand religion. It is because those who proclaim themselves as the true followers within all religions are not setting good examples, that so many people turn away from God. They fail to realize the great power that lies within them and therefore don't develop faith. This position also contributes directly to the conflict present in the world today.

All of the prophets meditated. There is a cave (in Mecca) in which it is said that the Prophet Muhammad used to meditate. Jesus was often seen sitting alone: We may say that he was talking to his Father or lost in love for his Father, or we may call it meditation. In our language, we call it meditation when we listen to God or commune with God by reciting holy words. When the Holy Word and the mind are united, this is meditation.

The thoughts that emerge in meditation are pure, true, and filled with love. It is very difficult to express these thoughts. It is like a mute trying to describe a sweet. How will he be able to praise the taste, as he is unable to speak?

It is essential that a person's mind should always be calm. Today there is so much material wealth, but there is no peace of mind. Meditation will bring peace to the troubled mind. Then peace will flow into society,

Look to whichever prophet you have faith in. Repeat whichever Holy Name you have faith in. Repeat it again and again and the dirt in your mind will be cleansed. The more we meditate, the cleaner our mind will become. Only then we will gain insight into what our prophets have preached.

At present we go to religious places listen, then come home and read religious books. But we should wonder why the virtues we have learned about have not become manifest in us. Why have we not become considerate toward others? Why have we not attained peace, or kindness, or love for others, or the desire to help others? It is because our minds are sick, and we are not taking the proper medicine for this illness.

All day we feed our bodies many different treats, but now we must recognize that there is also food for the mind. Our physical actions are guided by our mind. Our bodies follow whatever thought comes to our minds. Our hands and feet follow our mind's commands. We have no control over our thoughts. We feed our body all day, but don't provide food for our mind. When our minds receive the proper nourishment, we will not hurt anyone's feelings, we will not deprive anyone of their rights, and we will not become greedy. Our minds will turn in the direction which the Guru described when he said, "I see no one as an enemy, no one as a stranger; I get along with everyone." In every person we will see our Guru, our Father. After we meditate, our mind will perceive the Light of our Father in every person. Just by listening to God's Holy Name, we develop some better understanding.

We have another misconception: We do not give any importance to prophets other than our own. People have built a fort around their minds: "Our prophet is the greatest and there is no other like him." After meditation, you will realize that your Father, your prophet, never said that the others were inferior The prophet only speaks of God. He wants to see God in every leaf. The Messiah, the Nabi, the Prophets are very great, but they have all been sent by Him who is present in every leaf, to convey His messages. We have created these boundaries in our mind around the Nabi or Messiah. They never told us to construct them.

Why should we travel in such discomfort? Why not travel comfortably? We have taken a long and troubled journey – let us now continue our journey with ease. Ease will come through meditation, and we will realize what our prophets have emphasized: enlightenment will be illumined, and you will learn to love the leaves, the animals, the trees, the rivers – all of nature, the universe, and its Creator. Then the great fortresses of hatred we have built within us will begin to crumble. We need to understand the prophets' teachings and orders. This is not possible without meditation.

A flood of healing

The thoughts that arise within us comprise what we call the mind. Thoughts of anger, greed, and pride come from our mind. When we are able to control over our mind, we will not engage in actions that will harm our homes, our society, our country, or our friends. There will be peace all over, and there will be an aura of peace around every person.

Everything is within you. Peace is within you, and love is within you. There is also darkness within you. We need light to drive away this darkness. What is this light? Meditation. Meditation will give you the enlightenment that will unveil the light, and you will experience an indescribable power. You will only be able to say, "Wah! " Wah!" ("How great it is!")

When you meditate, your thoughts go towards one God – the One who is the Lord of the earth and the heavens. ,as the Prophet Muhammad says, the One who has given His light to all creation. Guru Gobind Singh describes a Power that permeates everything – in rivers, trees, mountains, in all countries.

Parmatma, the Supreme Soul, the Indestructible, the One who will live forever, the One who gives us our sustenance, the One who brings love and peace and courage, the One who teaches us to love and protect all is present everywhere.

God's messages are not for any one person, country, or race. Wherever people meditate, offer prayers to God, sing God's praises, or obey God's commands, that place becomes an ocean of peace from which a flood of healing arises to heal the leaves, the animals, the earth, and also human beings.

We have not yet made up our minds to accept that healing and blessing, and they are being wasted. The way to receive that blessing is through the path of meditation. You must concentrate and unite with the Almighty. Your mind will rise and unite with Him. Then wherever you may be, whether at home or in public, your mind will have risen above the challenges of daily life and it will not be affected, for it has reached that Place where all problems are being solved and the light of knowledge is perpetually being generated.

Today that light of knowledge exists. Many read sacred scriptures – be it the Holy Qur'an, the Guru Granth Sahib, the Bible, the Torah, or the Bhagavad Gita (world scriptures) – but their minds are not focused. How can we make the mind sit still? Through meditation. Then we will be healed. Our body and mind will always be in a state of joy. Then we will see Him everywhere, and He who is omnipotent will be ever present with us.

Do not think you can reason with your thoughts and thus control your mind. It is not possible. The mind will be at rest only when it receives its full nourishment through prayer and meditation. We wash our clothes, wash our bodies, and clean our houses, but we must also clean our minds. Guru Nanak says, "The mind is washed by meditation on God's Holy Name."

What are the signs of a clean mind? There is no evil in that person. His way of talking, of communicating with people, of sitting, everything will change, because the power of healing will have come into him. All who meet him will feel that healing power and sense of peace.

So from today on let us all go within ourselves. Many pray and go to religious places, but to deeply imbibe the teachings, we must meditate.

This is essential, because the mind is very hungry. If we do not feed it, it will become restless and irritable, nervous and intolerant.

Into the Light

When does a prophet come? A prophet comes when humanity enters darkness. He brings the knowledge of God, the Light of God, and the blessings of God. Then he grabs hold of people and leads them from darkness to Light. He guides those who are doing wrong to do good deeds.

Do not waste much time thinking. Do good. Remain faithful to whichever prophet or religion you are following, but it is essential to follow the orders of that prophet or religion. Now our actions are not worthy to be called their followers, so let us begin today to feed our hungry minds. This food will reach our mind only when we meditate and obey the rules that have been laid down.

We will only be able to obey them when we will meditate. Obedience is not in our hands; we do not have that power. All we can do is meditate. Through meditation, we will understand the enlightened wisdom of our prophets and their messages. Then when we have understood, our problems will be solved and our ailments will be healed. Once healed, we will be strong.

Without meditation, you will remain as you are. But with meditation, your conscience will speak from within you and clear your doubts. You will notice the changes in your life, the changes in your thoughts, as God's healing and love comes within you.

We must understand, accept, and obey, for we are not doing the work for which we took birth. We have brought great love, mercy, and virtues from God, but we are neither using them to nourish ourselves nor sharing them with society.

We have been praying for a long time, going to religious places for a long time, and many have died in the process without attaining peace. Let us change our ways, start to obey the commands, and banish this illness of the mind.

So let us meditate in order to come out of the darkness into the Light. Once we come into the Light, our countries and most importantly, we ourselves, will be at peace. We will receive great love and joy.

Only Nam Will Cleanse Your Mind

To the banjaras (Indian gypsies) who participated in an Amrit ceremony at Gobind Sadan

Guru Gobind Singh did such intensive meditation that he contemplated the Lord of Time and Death. Then from the state of duality, he became one with God. If you too, practice tapasya you can become great leaders. First comes tapasya, then the rest will follow.

The most important thing is to get up early every morning and meditate. The Guru said, "Kali Yuga has come. In Kali Yuga, only the God's Holy Name will save you. These times are very hot, and Nam is very cooling. The food of the mind is the Name of God. Without truth, you will be defiled. Your mind can be cleansed only with Nam." Then all the evils of your mind will go away, and the virtues will remain.

As your mind becomes clean, the actions of your body will also be cleansed. Our body is the instrument of our thoughts. When anger arises, the body shakes. To move in any direction, first the thought directs us moves that way, and then the body follows. Thus Maharaj says, "When the mind is conquered, you have conquered the world."

At present the mind is wavering twenty-four hours a day. But when the mind receives its full nourishment, full energy, then it becomes powerful. The ruler tried to kill the saintly sixteenth-century weaver, Kabir. Kabir said, "My mind is not frightened. How can you frighten the body?" Kabir was thrown before an elephant and placed in a fire; they tried to drown him and punished him by many means. He said only this: "You have tried your best. Your weapons are very sharp and your elephants very strong. But my mind is not frightened. How can you frighten the body? The body is made of dust, and the mind is not frightened. The mind does not see your elephants, nor your power. You have innumerable elephants and horses, but in my house, I have only one God with me. Please understand that my one God is more powerful than all your elephants, more powerful than your army and He is more powerful than you as well. I will pull you down at once, because God is more powerful than you." Then the king begged to be pardoned; Kabir had not asked to be pardoned. When he was bound by chains and thrown into the Ganges River, his fetters were broken by the waves of the Ganges, and she spread a deerskin for him to sit upon.

There is no limit to the greatness of Nam. The Guru says, "All living beings are sustained by Nam. This lower world and the higher world are all sustained by Nam; all regions of the universe are sustained by Nam." Thus the entire cosmos can be seen within you. The power of God will also be seen within you. Everything of God's will be seen within you; nothing is outside. When someone meditates, he is illumined from within; the Light comes from inside us. At that stage, caste is ended, distinctions of high and low are ended. One says, "Gobind, Gobind, Gobind," seeing Gobind (God) throughout the world.

Develop the habit of reciting Nam. The Fifth Guru says, "Do this while laughing, while standing, while dressing well, while eating – thus you will be liberated." Once you are joined with God, you will not be separated. This is God's habit: once He has taken your arm, you may try to shake Him off, but He will not let go of your arm. Even if you let go of His garment, He will remain with you; He will come again and again.

These days, there is fear, doubt, and selfishness in everyone's mind, for our base is unsteady. The mind is the base. How can we keep our mind powerful? Rise early in the morning. Thank God that He has given you sleep, has given you food. Arise and join with God. When you join with Him, there will be a shower of blessings, a flood of blessings. They are all created through Nam. Nam is a seed that gives birth to a tree under whose shade millions of people can rest and receive comfort. What tree is this? That which brings forth truthfulness, destroys evils, and puts an end to fear by creating fearlessness.

Live in the world as good people. Love, enlightenment, and compassion will arise within you, and your moral character will become very strong. At present there is one thing which everyone wants but they do not know how to obtain it. We are to get it from within. Sit and recite Nam, and you will receive it. It is a treasure which will never diminish.

Intoxication of Nam

A televised talk on drug addiction among the youth

A person's mind is not steady; it is always in motion. To stabilize the mind we take the help of dharam. Dharam feeds the hunger of the mind.

Why are children addicted to drugs today? Why have they lost their way? I feel the most important reason is that their role models have lost their way. In the old days, people used to follow dharam. Their minds were steady. They were of very high character, their thoughts were strong, and their hearts were very pure. Justice prevailed in their offices and in their courts. People were attracted toward dharam.

It is written in Guru Granth Sahib, "The food of the mind is the God's Holy Name; cherish it in your heart." Meditation is essential. As Guru Nanak said, "In the ambrosial early morning, chant the true Name of God and contemplate His greatness."

We think that perhaps by obtaining high positions and big houses, our mind will attain peace. To the contrary, they are not required for peace, and they usher in pride. The food that the mind needs is Nam. Our thoughts are scattered. Nam is necessary to collect our wandering thoughts and correct them. With Nam, steadiness, cheerfulness, and bliss will develop in the mind. The Guru observes, "When that taste comes, other tastes lose their appeal."

Today everyone should recite Nam and thus receive the aid of Nam. With the help of Nam, the mind will become steady and filled with the intoxication of enlightenment. Nothing else can make any impression on this state of mind. That Light is so powerful that it inevitably consumes ignorance. This was the intoxicant that Kabir felt. When he was thrown before an elephant, he felt no fear or danger. "My mind is not wavering," he said firmly.

"How can you frighten my body?" As it is written in the Guru Granth Sahib, "By reciting the Name of the Fearless One, all fears are ended. The Fearless One abides with you; how can fear arise?

Today there is no trace of fearlessness even in those who serve in our religious places. Priests have been installed in every religion. In the Sikh tradition, the priests are called granthis, for they read the scripture (Guru Granth Sahib).

Granthis existed even in the time of Guru Gobind Singh, but there is a great difference between them and today's granthis. The granthis of old opened the scripture and read passages in the same manner as is done today. But transformation does not come simply from reading the scripture. Transformation occurs only when you obey the orders. If you do not follow the guidance, it makes no difference whether you bow your head before the scripture or not. As the Guru says, "One gains approval by obeying the commandments, and reaches God's palace."

We may ask a priest to pray for us, but not everyone's prayer is answered. As it is written in the Guru Granth Sahib, "The prayer of a true devotee always bears fruit. Only the prayers of wise and noble persons are answered. Baba Deep Singh was a granthi who led an army of villagers to restore the sanctity of the Golden Temple after it had been desecrated by invading kings. He prayed to God that his head should not fall until he reached the Golden Temple. However, his head was severed in battle as they fought their way toward the Temple. Baba Deep Singh picked up his head with one hand and kept fighting with his sword in the other hand. He had so much faith that when he fell short of the Temple, he threw his head from a great distance away and it landed in the inner precincts of the Temple. Today temples still stand to mark the place of this great miracle. Such was the life of a granthi of old; those whose prayers were answered. He is considered the greatest among the martyrs, for he was the bravest of donors; he gave his head.

The Guru Granth Sahib says that a person with faith in Dharam attains three positions: He is a giver, a devotee, and a brave person. Baba Deep Singh took all three awards. He was a true granthi, a true follower.

Nowadays we take guidance from the scripture per our own choice, and interpret it according to our own needs and desires. Thus people have lost their way.

How can we find our way? As Guru Nanak says, "May I feel the ecstasy of Nam day and night." When you become intoxicated by Nam, you will become brave. You will not be affected by worldly intoxicants. Nam will take you to such a level that if your body is being cut into pieces, Nam will still go on and the effect of that intoxication will not be diminished. As Bhai Mati Das's body was being sawn into two, one half was repeating the final lines of Guru Nanak's Jap ji Sahib, "Those who meditate on the Name of God have earned the reward for their rigorous efforts when they depart," and the other half was completing the phrase, "Oh Nanak, their faces glow with Light, and many more are liberated along with them." The saw blade became tired, but the sound of Gurbani continued. What was that intoxication? The intoxication of full concentration on Nam.

Today's youth are looking for some shelter, and running after drugs and alcohol. Worldly intoxicants are ruining their bodies, whereas intoxication with Nam makes people courageous. Light streams from their faces and they are enthusiastically greeted in heaven. Thus they become immortal. Nam brings the light of enlightenment, and fear departs. The person will become brave, and love and faith will develop. He will feel that his Guru is always by his side to protect him, that He is nearer than his own hands and feet, and visible with every breath.

People are forsaking religion, for the religious leaders are not following religious principles. If they would set an example people would follow. If all of us start following the principles, there will be a flood of good people everywhere. People will be encouraged to rejoin that stream. Now when we urge the youth to follow the leaders, they begin criticizing them. We must remind our youth of those people of older times who were true granthis and ragis (devotional singers). The day our youth are satisfied, addiction to drugs will be eradicated not only in Punjab but in the whole world.

Today we listen to the scripture being recited but we do not practice its teachings. Once when Guru Gobind Singh was giving audience, one Sikh was reciting the passage from Jap ji Sahib (Guru Nanak's preamble to Guru Granth Sahib), "Indescribable is the state of the true believer. Whosoever attempts to speak of it will ultimately regret his folly. Pen and paper can never capture it, even though many may sit and contemplate it. Such is the greatness of God's Holy Name, but only those who truly believe it in their heart can realize it." A wise person was listening and continually questioning the one praying, "What does it matter to you?" The reader complained to the Guru that the other man was disturbing his prayers.

When the man was questioned, he replied, "Maharaj, when he was reading he was not paying attention. I just said to him, 'You are not practicing what you are reading, so what does it matter to you? Why are you wasting your time?"

Maharaj Guru Gobind Singh said, "You are correct. If you are not practicing, there is no use in reciting scripture."

If you practice what is written, your life changes, your character is elevated. The true follower who practices meditation cannot be described, for as it is written in the Guru Granth Sahib, "The true follower of God is like God."

A person may be chanting, "Ram, Ram," but his attention may be somewhere else. If one's attention and Nam are joined, then as Bhagat Kabir said, "My mind has become pure as the water of the Ganges, and Ram is following me, saying 'Kabir, Kabir." Kabir says, "I am reciting the same 'Ram' that other people recite, but He can be seen in my deeds. People are cured, whereas nothing happens when others chant 'Ram.' People apply a sacred mark on their forehead and worship with flowers, but they are simply carrying out rituals." As it is written in the Guru Granth Sahib, "People look upon God as a plaything and just copy each other; they cannot attain God." They do not understand the purpose of their actions.

A person who passes the test of God becomes like Kabir, Nam Dev, Trilochan, Dhanna (great saints whose hymns are enshrined in Guru Granth Sahib). To become intoxicated like them, you must take God's shelter, you must take God's blessings. The cure of addiction to drugs lies not with doctors but with God alone. As it is written, "From the day that God casts His merciful gaze upon you, you will be filled with happiness." Within us will come Light, enlightenment, love, attraction to God. The Fifth Guru says, "The love of God can neither be torn nor severed, so strong is its pull."

By contrast, we are always complaining. We always criticize God, saying, "I have been waiting so long, but my wish has not been fulfilled." What happened in those places where historic gurdwaras have been built? At Sis Ganj (where the Ninth Guru gave his head to preserve Hindus' right to religious freedom), many were martyred, to ensure our happiness and comfort. So many heads were sacrificed there that the place is called "Sis Ganj" (the place where heads were cut off). When we read our prayers, we say, "If you recite the name of the Ninth Guru, prosperity will come in your home." Do not expect this prosperity – first you too must give your head. All kinds of happiness will definitely come, but first you must sacrifice your self in service to God.

Anandpur Sahib (Guru Gobind Singh's citadel) is the site of great struggles, hard times, and sacrifices. But Guru Gobind Singh always felt anand (bliss). When he sacrificed his children, he enjoyed the state of bliss. When he gave his mother and father, he still felt blissful. When his clothes were torn and he had no shoes, he still felt blissful. We go to Anandpur Sahib and shout His praises, but how was it built?

Today we go there and ask the sewadar (devotees who serve the community) to give us karah prasad – blessed offering. He can give us only the food, not blessings. We could prepare the food at home. God's blessings come from following the commandments. Guru Gobind Singh always used to say "Tav prasad" – "God, it is Your blessing." When receiving water, when receiving food, before putting on shoes, before mounting a horse, he always thanked God.

We, too, must practice religion in our own lives. Then righteousness will spread throughout the world. If instead we go to religious gatherings, gossip, bow our head, and go home, how will dharam spread? The Guru has said, "What good is merely bowing the head when the heart is impure? Criminals also stoop low, as do deer hunters." A hunter may lie low for hours, but he has no concern for God. Your personality will not change simply by bowing your head as a hunter does.

Today's youth observe the behaviour of the religious leaders and are not impressed with them for they do not follow dharma. They look at today's religious leaders and do not see a Baba Deep Singh. They see the lives of today's granthis and ragis. Youth will only leave intoxicants when they see good examples.

We must take the intoxication of dharam. Other intoxicants will bring only destruction. Corruption and lying will spread. We will commit injustice and be of low character, because our mind will waver under the effect of worldly intoxicants. If we become intoxicated with Nam, dharam will prevail.

Guru Gobind Singh gave Khalsa the mask of a lion and told them to practice spiritual principles, to renounce anger, criticism, and lust, and to be attached to Nam. He warned them that they should never allow their character to weaken. Maharaj says that once you take off the mask of a lion, your value will end. Your spiritual power will vanish, and people will see that this mask has been removed and that nobody is following the commandments. This is the reason why addiction is so widespread and why everyone has become weak.

Now we must practice dharam, we must follow the Masters' commandments. With this, worldly intoxication and corruption will end, and well-being will return.

Forsake Anger, Not God

A telephone talk to the sangat (congregation) in Gobind Sadan, U.S.A.

Religion never teaches us to be angry with anyone, or to be jealous, or to deprive anyone of his rights. We have always been trained to understand that, as Guru Nanak says, "We are all brothers and sisters; no one is a stranger." Guru Nanak says that God is omnipresent, that His Love, His Light, and His blessings are to be found in every leaf. Guru Gobind Singh said, "God is in the waters, God is in the earth, God is in the caves, God is in the mountains." He taught us only love, emphasizing that his followers should first forsake anger. A person who truly imbibes religious teachings has no anger. Guru Gobind Singh pointed out that a person who becomes free of anger becomes so powerful that he sees God in every human being and sees God and God's blessings in the whole light-filled creation.

The Prophet Muhammad likewise said, "The One whom I call Allah is the Master of the earth and skies of the whole universe. When Allah is forgiving, then why are humans so vengeful?" Jesus also taught us love, in a very sweet voice. He said that a person who prays according to the Bible will never take away anyone's rights but will rather give love. He will not be angry toward anyone; he will think of him with compassion.

In our various countries, some go to gurdwaras, some to church, some to temple, some to mosque, but none of these places teach us anger and hatred. The church teaches us to look for the Father's light, love, and mercy in everyone. The temple likewise, teaches, as Lord Ram said, that as much as possible, we are to love every human being and love all of nature.

Religion is not something to be learned intellectually; it is experienced within us. When enlightenment comes, a light shines from within revealing that everything is God. Then one sees God in the earth, the skies, in the whole universe. When God is seen throughout the universe, then why should there be hatred? Why fear? Why criticism?

We humans have not come here to oppose any of the prophets or Messiahs; we have come to receive their blessings. The Prophet Muhammad revealed that God produced everything that you need – your food, drinking water, material for houses and daily life – but God kept one thing to Himself. He then sent that to us through the prophets and Messiahs. Guru Gobind Singh, for instance, removed the fear, cowardice, and greed from within us.

He cleansed our minds with his power and his enlightenment and we began to help the weak, feed the poor, and serve everyone, even by sacrificing our own lives. Weakness is not a matter of caste, but of feebleness of mind and body. Meditation strengthens the mind. Prayer also strengthens the mind because it removes the thorns that have become attached to it. Our ego, our greed are great thorns pricking our minds. All the prophets and Messiahs came to spread their light and remove these thorns that prick us.

However, today these thorns of greed, anger, and desire dominate us because we are not following the inner power which makes us obey God's teachings. We do whatever comes to our mind. Guru Nanak says that our mind comes under control only when God's full blessing falls upon us. To receive that blessing, we have to pray, we have to meditate.

Houses of worship must demonstrate dharam. As Guru Gobind Singh said, the gurdwara is not a place for quarreling, or of criticism, or of anger. It is a place where the tenth door (the portal to the spiritual realm) is opened for you, and your ignorance is removed. He says that nine doors (the physical entrances to the body) were shown to you, but the tenth door was kept a mystery. It is through the tenth door that one can see God in everything. When the tenth door is opened, then we see that everywhere there is Gobind, everywhere there is God, everywhere there is Allah; we see our Father everywhere. But instead, we have rebelled against the teachings of our prophets everywhere.

Let us today go back and see what teachings our prophets have given us. Jesus taught us love, service, and humility. The Prophet Muhammad told us that Allah teaches us to love, that a person who is greedy and angry will not benefit from Allah's blessings. Allah will bless those who love from the heart and who want to serve.

Guru Gobind Singh taught that the Khalsa, the pure, are those who have given up evil intentions – that in one's very gaze there should be forgiveness and love. He removed all barriers of caste and creed, high and low, saying "Recognize all people as one human race." He saw God in everyone, and taught that we should love all people and treat them with respect. Give them food and clothing as we would welcome any fellow human being. The Prophet Muhammad also placed great emphasis on hospitality. He said if a guest comes to your home, welcome him, feed him lovingly, and wash his feet.

The loving family and lovely children of Guru Gobind Singh were sacrificed because he wanted to teach everyone to live in harmony, to make every voice strong, and to provide religious freedom to everyone. When there was great pressure on the people, Jesus sacrificed himself on the cross to teach us all to love, to serve, and to bring everyone to sit together and see the Light. The Prophet Muhammad sacrificed his loving family to show us not to oppress anyone – to look for that light in everyone. Moses gave up everything including the kingdom and throne in order to free his enslaved people, those whose voices were suppressed and who were being forced to obey the rulers.

Each one of us, each country now needs to recognize love. We should all think of the time when Jesus was being crucified. We should all think back to the time when Guru Gobind Singh's young sons were being buried alive in a wall, and when he left his home in Anandpur Sahib. No man has ever been born who could force him to leave, but he was teaching us that even if it is necessary to leave your house for the good of people and for the sake of righteousness, then leave your house. If you need to give up your life for the love of people, for the freedom of people, for the good of people, then give up your life. The examples which they set should not be ignored, for it will not be good for us if we do so. Until we get rid of anger, there will be no love, and no blessings from the prophets on our societies, our homes, our countries.

Today we are challenging our prophets. Everyone who goes to church should speak of love; those who go to the mosque should speak of love, those who follow Buddha should speak of love. All have taught us love, enlightenment, and devotion. I appeal to everyone with love and humility, not as a master, but as one of you, because I feel we are all following the wrong path.

Anger is very bad. It breaks up homes, causes illness in the mind, and creates enemies. Forsake anger and accept the love given by Jesus, by the Prophet Muhammad, by Guru Gobind Singh, by all the prophets. They came to cleanse our minds. We go to their holy places, yet we do not obey their commands. We kneel and bow our heads, but our souls are still not cleansed. If we bow our heads and pray but do not renounce anger, then our prayers are flawed for they are devoid of love. If we go to a gurdwara and still feel anger, Guru Gobind Singh has not blessed us. He is showering His blessings twenty-four hours a day. It is we who have closed the doors and windows of our mind and our inner wisdom. Open them. Clean your minds so that the prophets' blessings will fall upon a pure mind, so that they will look at you lovingly and bestow upon you their love and willingness to serve. Instead they are all annoyed with us because they did so much for us – they hung on the cross, they sacrificed their children, they gave up their reign – but still we are opposing them.

Guru Gobind Singh is thinking, "I have said that Khalsa forsakes anger, greed, and criticism. Was there some weakness in my way of speaking, or is the weakness in those who claim to believe in me?" When he thinks this way, we should feel very ashamed, for the weaknesses are in us, not in him. Is not Jesus thinking, "I have explained to them very well, but what has happened to them? Why are they so belligerent? Why are they taking up artillery guns and shells? I have told them that if a person slaps you on one cheek, you should turn the other cheek to him as well." The Prophet Muhammad may also be thinking, "People are attacking each other now, but I have told them that when we think of Allah, we are all brothers. A Muslim has a soft heart. He is full of mercy and love, and is always receiving the Light of Allah."

The Prophet is love, Guru Gobind Singh is love, Jesus is love, Moses is love. Hatred is not theirs; it is something which we have created. It is said that this is the work of Satan. Have you all become followers of Satan? You must become followers of the God who has blessed you with love and forgiveness. Pray, "Oh God, why has Satan become so powerful over us? Drive him away." When you pray with your heart, the devil will run away. Concentrate on Guru Gobind Singh and the devil will run away. Satan is there only when the Guru is not casting his merciful gaze upon you, when you are not receiving the love of the Messiah or the Prophet.

You are hiding behind ignorance. If you look with enlightened vision, love is raining down upon us. Accept that love. I appeal to all countries, all castes, all religions, and I pray to God: "Oh God, please give enlightenment to all those who are today challenging Your commandments." God is not happy with us now because we are going against His will, as explained by the prophets. Save yourselves! Be very careful, because you do not know what is going to happen because of this anger.

Today let us all return to our prophets, to our God. We are all drifting away from them. We are defying Him, and by defying Him, we will never find contentment. There will be no peace on our earth, in our skies, and in our minds. Our countries and our minds will all become upset. Our prosperity will be impeded; people will become ill. Their minds will be sad and their souls suppressed. If your soul is burdened, what was the use of the prophets' coming? So let us all repent and sorrowfully pray, "Oh Father, please control our minds. Forgive us our many mistakes."

Today you are not just fighting with human beings; you have challenged the prophets and their teachings. Let us all save ourselves and follow the path of our prophets. Otherwise, lock up your mosques, your churches, your gurdwaras, so that you do not go there to challenge them. If you want to open these locks, then obey all their commandments.

Let us sit together and consider the results of our anger. Let us solve matters peacefully and with love. If there is a quarrel in your home, resolve it. If there is a fight in your country, solve it. Solutions can be found with love. Anger destroys everything.

An uncontrolled mind makes many mistakes. When a person makes mistakes, he loses, his society suffers, and the thinking of the country changes. When there are quarrels within families, homes break up and the children are scarred. Fighting has never been beneficial.

Let us not compete over who is the strongest. Only God is strong. Therefore love God and take His blessings to become strong. That person is strong who has within him the wealth of truth, love, humility, and service. It is for this that our prophets sacrificed, became martyrs, and gave up their families: to tell us that he alone is great who loves God, who loves God's creation, who adores all His things. So let us all become great people.

Please Listen to Your Alarm

A message for the third anniversary of
H.H. Acharya Sushil Kumar

From time immemorial, Jain monks, nuns, and Tirthankaras (incarnations or avtars within the Jain tradition) have emphasized Ahimsa (the principle of non-violence). Every prophet has taught that we should not cause injury to others. But even today, after all these teachings, we are failing to practice it fully. Aggressive actions are not the only form of violence; we injure others by our speech and our thoughts as well.

Once this inner violence is controlled, whenever you look at someone, love will arise within them. Whenever you speak to someone, love will arise within them. But now this inner violence does not allow you any peace, and your very tongue speaks violently. It is possible that this force of violence is within you all. Make an effort to cast it out, through meditation.

We have been given a very sensitive thermometer by which our innermost thoughts and feelings are always being measured. This thermometer is equipped with an alarm which rings to alert us to the slightest bad thought or action. When we merely move our hand forward to commit some wrong action, the alarm rings. When we merely begin to think in an evil way, it rings. But we are not ready to listen to our own alarm. Instead, we are forever listening to other people's alarms. Please listen to your own alarm, which is ringing day and night, "Tunn, tunn, tunn!" The noise of this alarm is so loud that it doesn't even allow you to sleep at night. If an angry thought arises, immediately the alarm rings and asks, "Why is it necessary to be angry?" The alarm keeps clanging, but people have become so dull-witted that they have stopped listening. Our inner alarms may even be breaking down because they have become tired of making so much noise.

If we have any grievance against anyone, we must immediately sit and look inside ourselves to ask, "Is the fault that I am attacking in this other person also inside me? If it is in me, first I must remove it from myself. By then, perhaps I will not see that fault in the other person. Instead of fighting with him, the battle will be raging within me." If you do this, truth will finally be victorious. It will raise the battle cry, vanquish the inner wickedness, cast it out, and then retire to its camp to rest. Once we eliminate our own inner darkness, we are sure to see the light in the other person.

At present, our thoughts are out of control. Thought races so fast that no one has been able to measure its speed. Only one thing can brake its speed: meditation. The person who is able to apply the brakes to thought can diminish its effect. Then the power of violence will come to an end, and the power of love will begin."

Purify the Mind: An Urgent Global Appeal

Everyone's mind has slipped off its base. This is not a problem of one particular country or culture; everyone's mind is wavering.

What do I mean by the mind? Our thoughts. The day that you gain control over your thoughts, you will have control over your anger, control over your feelings of enmity, and control over your self-centeredness. This is very necessary at present. All people need to control their minds.

We all keep on saying, "Love and have faith. Love your brother and sister, love your friend, love your co-workers, love animals, love the trees." We merely continue to mouth these words, but the prophets who have given these messages have truly loved.

Why don't we love? Because our thoughts are out of control. Every prophet who came has given this message: "Control your mind." Some have said "Worship." Some have said "Pray." Some have said "Recite scripture." Some said, "Do puja (Hindu)." But all these exhortations are about one thing: how to control our thoughts.

When people lost control over their thoughts, they were not able to recognize Jesus, because anger had intervened. If they had control over their minds, they could never have attacked Jesus. When anger arises, a person goes out of control. Anger and ego make a person unconscious. If you become conscious, the whole world will rejoice.

Now we are all insisting on clean air. This is fine. But who has polluted the air? People whose thoughts are angry, whose thoughts are uncontrolled. When a person's thoughts change, he commits crimes, usurps others' rights, hurts others' feelings.

All of us, in every country, in every home, in every society, have the same disease. What is the cure for this disease? You must act upon the message which our masters, our prophets have given. Then your mind will be controlled.

Jesus never taught us to commit crimes, to usurp others' rights, to hurt others' feelings. Neither did the Prophet Muhammad. They taught only love and worship. Guru Gobind Singh's teachings were the same. He went so far as to say, "See God in the water, in the land, in the mountains, in the forests, in people's minds." He also said that if we damage an object it can be repaired afterward, but if a person's feelings are injured, perhaps they cannot be repaired.

Why has anger arisen in some societies and countries at this time? Our minds are not controlled. When poisonous speech, poisonous anger issue forth from a person, that terrible poison enters the air. It rises though the trees and spreads in circles. The poison in the atmosphere is so strong that a person commits crime, hurts others' feelings, deprives others of their rights. He attacks good people – this is the most toxic thought of all.

Control your mind and your mouth, and other things will be controlled automatically. In the beginning, God created very fresh air, fresh trees to shade us, fresh mountains, fresh water. Who has contaminated them? The poisonous thoughts of self-centered individuals.

Therefore all our countries need to feed the mind that food which will bring forth compassion, love, and willingness to serve. When will these arise? When we act upon the sayings of the prophets. They have said if you would love trees, know that flowers also want love. If you would love flowers, know that the earth also wants love.

The Prophet Muhammad said, 'My Allah is in the whole creation. Love all of creation." Jesus said,, "Love the flowers, because my Father is within them, within the trees, within the mountains." Guru Gobind Singh said the same.

Therefore we should first act upon the sayings of our prophets, and talk less. Our loving thoughts should burn away the poisonous voice which comes from within. Only good thoughts should come from us, for they are pure. When only thoughts of love emerge, then thoughts of compassion will appear, and thoughts of service will prevail over thoughts of enmity. I have firm faith in God that our countries' conflicts and the breaking of boundaries between countries will then end.

Upon becoming good human beings, we should carefully consider this: on the one hand our countries are spending millions of rupees to annihilate people and on the other hand we are spending great amounts to build hospitals to treat people. On one side we are killing, and on the other side we are saving lives. What is this? People do not have enough money to spend on such things. The people want food, they want houses, clothes, good education. Give those to the people. Just control these double expenditures, and perhaps the things which the people need may rush forth.

We are all eating the wrong food

I am sharing with you only that which will benefit our countries, bring peace to our minds, bring unity within our families, and bring forth thoughts of serving others. You should all take this food. We are all eating the wrong food.

Worldly food affects the body but has no effect on our thoughts. What food does the mind require? Truth. Love. Desire to serve. Compassion. When these arise in the mind, we will not need lectures. The very air will speak automatically, once the poisonous air is cleansed by good air. It is like putting detergent into dirty clothes to remove the dirt. Once the filth is separated from the clothes, they become shining clean.

At this time, the shine is needed. Our countries will shine when there is compassion, love and equality.

We are now giving everyone the wrong food. I therefore appeal to all of you that we must eat the right food. If we go to a church, we should obey the commandments of the church. If we go to a gurdwara, we should obey the commandments of the gurdwara. All religious places are made for us to clean the mind and bring forth love within the mind.

When the wind or water is out of control, great damage occurs. If the control over our thoughts is broken, understand that ever greater damage will ensue.

At present, we have lost control over our thoughts. So I am appealing to all of you who are reading or listening to this message, and I am also praying before God, "Please bring forth that compassion which is in Your Kingdom. Please bring forth that peace which is in Your Kingdom."

We should all give voice to those qualities we ourselves require. If we speak with anger, anger will come back to us from others.

It is not essential to have long lines of people going in to bow in churches and gurdwaras. Why? These places are training schools to purify our thoughts. Instead, we go there, bow our heads, and return home the same as we were before. There is nothing lacking in our masters or in the training they have given us. The deficiency is in our minds. You should leave a place of worship only after purifying your mind. If God's Light comes, it should fall upon a clean mind, and you should nurture it. If the mind is so dirty, where will that pure Light come?

The master says, "Worship. Recite scripture. Pray. Do puja." We should all take this food by acting upon this guidance. To worship with love, pray with love, read scripture with love is to give the mind the right food. Guru Nanak said again and again that in this age, the food of the mind is God's Holy Name. Without nam, our evils cannot be removed.

The commandments of our masters – those whom we accept as our teachers, whom we feel are the deliverers of God's message – are also food for the mind. However, we must act according to their commandments. When we go to a place of worship, we are told to speak truth and not to tell lies. If we go to a place of worship and still tell lies, we are not obeying the commandments. If we hurt others' feelings or usurp their rights, we are not obeying the commandments. If we follow the commandments, our mind and body will be happy, and we will not be worried. When the master enters the picture, then we are free.

Always set aside your ego. A person is never willing to do so. He insists, "I am!" But our teachers have emphasized that ego is not a good thing, for it is the opposite of remembering God, the opposite of love. Ego and love cannot coexist.

I have faith in goodness

I have firm faith that the qualities of compassion, love, service, and sharing which are within human beings will come forth in all of us. Guru Gobind Singh began using a very powerful word, "Khalsa", to describe those people whose minds have become inwardly pure. He said, "Who is Khalsa? One who renounces anger. One who renounces criticizing others. One who renounces adultery." Further, he said that Khalsa is one who loves the Name of God, is joined with God, and also links others with God."

Jesus said, "Those who love me should love the whole creation." The Prophet Muhammad said the same thing, and so did Moses. Moses left the kingdom which was to be his, for the sake of those who were weak. He was to become king and marry the princess, but he left the kingdom and fine carriages and began traveling barefoot. He prayed, "Oh God, this is my request: Please give these people good food, end their slavery, and give them good homes." God became so happy that He made Moses a prophet. Why? Because God is so merciful that when you have compassion for others, God will give you oceans of compassion; God will make you master of compassion.

Consider the staff which God blessed for Moses. As you all know, that staff had great powers. When Moses cast it toward the sea, the sea split into two parts. Anyone may carry a stick, but that particular stick was blessed by God because it was in the hands of Moses.

Similarly, whatever Guru Gobind Singh touched became pure. The same is true of the cloth which touched the body of Jesus. Even today, love emerges from the cloth and enters the body of those who see it.

Therefore, all of us should eat the right food. The air is clean, but we have polluted it. The water is clean, but we have polluted it. Society is also clean, but we have polluted it. We must all take great care, for this has gone on for a very long time.

We must decide

Since on one hand, money is being spent on hospitals, and on the other, money is being spent on weapons, we should first sit and decide whether we should make these double expenditures. If poisonous things are not created, a person will never become sick. There will be no need for hospitals. Why? A human being is himself healthy. In the time of Noah, of Abraham, of Moses, there were no hospitals, for their thoughts were pure. The trees of that time were also purified after listening to their thoughts. The air and earth likewise became pure after listening to the thoughts of the prophets.

We must make one decision: to do no wrong. Why? Too much pressure has been put on the world. Guru Gobind Singh sacrificed all his family members for the sake of one point: "Love, love, love." The Prophet Muhammad's family members were sacrificed for "Love, love, love." All of Jesus's disciples and many of his early followers were sacrificed, and they were all of one voice: "Love, love, love."

All prophets were repeating, "There is one God, one God, one God." Some called that God "Father." Some called that God "Friend." Guru Nanak who spoke of God in all relationships, Father, Mother, Brother, Sister, Friend, even said to God at one point, "You are my true Girlfriend." He saw that our love of God encompasses all relationships.

Women have been greatly praised in God's House, where a woman is number one. When God selects a prophet, first God selects a mother to give birth to the prophet.

We humans have made sectarian religions, but the messages of all prophets are one. Guru Gobind Singh called God "Father" and so did Jesus. Calling God "Father" does not alter the nature of God. Truly, God is Father of us all.

The greatest thing is that all of us should love. We should not draw tight circles around religions. Why? The various religions are different disciplines. We do not even practice the disciplines, but we are all sitting here trying to create conflicts between religions.

Guru Gobind Singh had no boundaries. He said, "God is the Sustainer and also the Merciful One, the Creator and also the Compassionate One. Temple and mosque are the same. Puja and Namaz are the same. We are all God's human beings. We are all members of one race: humanity. Don't love on the basis of separate religions or castes. Love others as fellow human beings."

Today we all need this. With great love, I appeal to you all. I have firm faith that perhaps after you listen to this, God will make you feel from inside that we should accept goodness and discard that which is bad. Guru Nanak has said, "Share virtues and forsake evils." Now we have shared the bad and forsaken the good.

Waste no time

At present there is a huge bonfire raging. Only our love, our pure thoughts can extinguish it. But day by day, anger is entering our thoughts. To the extent that enmity increases, to that extent the mind cannot be cleaned. Thought is the most poisonous of all things. Clean it.

Our mind which has gone out of control must be controlled, and we must give it the food which the prophets have given us. Their commandments are valid even today. They themselves are blessed, and those who follow their commandments are blessed.

Guru Ram Das, the fourth Sikh Guru says, "My Master is everlasting. He neither comes nor goes. He is immortal and is all pervading." Jesus says, "God is present." The Prophet Muhammad says, "He is present in whatever you see." Guru Gobind Singh says, "He is present and luminously apparent; see Him." If we do not believe, we are unaware of His presence. Guru Gobind Singh says to God, "You are present and always visible within human beings. You are always the Giver of pure thoughts to a person and also the person's Purifier."

Today there is a great need to bring your thoughts under control. Everyone has lost control over their thoughts. Don't emphasize lectures.

Dharam is not a matter of books or lectures. It is a matter of inner action. Your actions should speak, not your tongue. In your movements there should be compassion and love and willingness to serve.

So many conferences are being held on the subject of uniting all religions. But religion is already one. All prophets say that religion is truth, love, and service. You have made religions separate. Don't speak about uniting them; become one from within. Millions of rupees are being wasted on conferences, and people are wasting their lives and time buying tickets and attending them. Just sit in your home and carefully look at God within yourself. He is sitting inside you.

Meetings will not tell you about God. Those whom God sent to instruct us were illiterate. Jesus did not go to school to study, for he came to earth after completing his studies in heaven. Guru Nanak never went to school. The Prophet Muhammad referred to himself as "oomi," illiterate. It is not a matter of schooling; it is a matter of love. Take it readily, all of you. You need not pay anything; it is free. God is waiting to give it to you. Do not compete with God or ignore God's commandments. God is very merciful. Take mercy from the Merciful One. Take compassion from the Compassionate One. Take love from the Loving One.

The Ninth Sikh Guru said, "Why are you going to the forests to find Him? Search for Him within yourselves." Saint Nam Dev, when he saw God, said, "All is Gobind (God), all is Gobind. Look at the trees; He is sitting there. Look at the earth, look at the heavens – Gobind is sitting there. Gobind is within you." All of you should turn within and forsake enmity. The energy which you are wasting should be directed toward God.

I am only writing you about those things which your masters, your gurus, have already told you. I am not imposing anything new from my side. I am just reminding you that we should all obey our prophets' commands.

Those who have directed their thoughts toward goodness became saints. Those who focused their thoughts became good scientists, good professors, and they were very useful in the world. At present, we are all wasting our thoughts. What is this? Are we all angry with God? Are we not challenging God, saying "We will do the opposite of whatever You have said"? Why can't we see God in every particle? We are just bowing our heads and not obeying Him. Merely bowing our heads, we have become old. Now obey Him! A long time has passed.

We should all beg forgiveness and take the blessings of God. We have committed many mistakes. Whatever mistakes we have committed, we should all repent and ask for pardon. Whatever good things God has given to us, we should use them for the sake of goodness.

Forsake anger, now! Love God. If our master says, "Forsake anger," we should not fight with him. If he says, "Forsake anger," then forsake it. It is not a big thing. We have wasted so much time. The time which we have wasted will not return. Take care now, all of you.

As Guru Ram Das says, "Oh my life, do not delay even for a moment. There is no certainty whether the next breath will come or not." But you are wasting time. God's doors are open. But you should be ready to accept what your Father is ready to give you.

As Guru Nanak has said, "There is one Father, and we are all His children." The one whom we call Father is the Father of the whole creation. We should become as members of one family, and obey the Father.

Inner Non-Violence

To the participants of The International Pilgrimage for Peace and Life

Who is responsible for peace or violence? Human beings. To bring peace and end violence, we each have to turn within ourselves and bring peace therein. Peace is an inner thing. It cannot be obtained by marching or reading books or by delivering lectures. We must not advertise goods which we do not possess.

The violence in our actions may be obvious. But even when we speak egotistically, we commit violence. To think bad thoughts is also violence. We must first control these things.

When someone commits violence, the very air becomes disturbed; the land, the trees, the animals become upset. Unless we turn within ourselves, we will never see God in the trees, in the animals, in the earth, and our mind will never leave its fortress.

When Lord Buddha was enlightened, he said "Do not commit violence." He said that when he saw Light everywhere. Likewise, when Jesus saw God everywhere with enlightened vision, he also said, "It is necessary to love people, but at the same time love the flowers, the trees, the animals, the whole Creation." But when did he speak? When he was enlightened.

Similarly, Hazrat Muhammad once said, "Love Allah, but also love human beings and love the land, because Allah's Light is everywhere." But when did he speak? When he became one with that Great Power.

Likewise, one day Guru Gobind Singh said from his state of enlightenment, "God is in the water, God is in the earth, God is in the cave, God is in the mountain." He said, "That which is God gives His Light and Truth to every place and takes care of the whole Creation."

Similarly, Guru Nanak said, "God is not limited to one country; God is not only in one place. God gives Light and Love to the whole Creation. Just behold Him clearly." And Lord Krishna once said, "Look with the eyes of your soul. There is nothing which is not within your soul. His Light, His Love are everywhere. Don't make boundaries, don't stress sectarian divisions. Stress the universality of Creation."

Heal your mind first

Once Guru Teg Bahadur (Ninth Sikh Guru), in his wisdom, spoke of the violence in our subconscious which precedes thought and speech. He said, "Beware even of achet paap (subconscious sin) which hasn't even entered your consciousness."

Our mind is like a wild horse – our thoughts, our desires are not under our control. We are all in need of enlightened wisdom and healing. I think if we all fight against our bad thoughts from morning to night, we will be so busy that we will have no time to hurt others or even speak with anger.

Look what we do: We hold big seminars, big lectures, and speak about peace based on what we have learned from books. The prophets also always spoke about peace, but what is the difference between us and the prophets? They were already healed. They spoke from inner enlightenment, and thus their words, their gaze, and their thought had a power which was transmitted to others.

Lord Buddha did not speak in fancy buildings. He spoke everywhere, and whenever he spoke, he had an impact on the minds of the people. All of them then wanted to grow in love, spiritual enlightenment, and service. Similarly, Lord Jesus did not speak in big buildings or hold big seminars. Whenever he encountered a conflict along the way, he healed it. He also healed the trees beneath which he stood. Why? Because the power of God which always heals everything had come within him. Inside us is a very great Power which we do not see.

Now all of us should look inside ourselves, just for one minute, and ask, "Is there anyone among us who has never been angry? Anyone who is not filled with pride"? I think anger and ego have overcome every one. The day when we gain control over our own bad thinking – even two or four people – then perhaps there will be no violence in the whole world and love will develop within us.

This is not just a matter of speaking. Once Guru Nanak was sitting beneath a tree whose fruit was very bitter – in Punjab we call this tree soap-nut, "raitha." Mardana said to him, "I'm hungry." Guru Nanak said, "Never mind. Eat this fruit." Mardana replied, "It's very bitter." Maharaj ordered, "No. Now its bitterness has gone away. It has been healed and it has become sweet." Even today that tree still stands as proof. And when the fruit of that tree falls, it is still sweet. Why? Whatever thought comes into our mind, whatever word comes to our tongue, whatever action we take goes out into the whole environment.

Break the boundaries

Whenever great spiritual personalities have met God and then spoken, they have never said, "I have come for one country, for just a few people." They have spoken for the whole universe. But what have we all done? We have made forts and made each prophet the leader of a party.

Having made these boundaries, on the one hand we say, "Don't commit violence," and on the other hand we criticize other religions. That is also violence. To hurt others' feelings is violence as well. First we must all reject the violence within ourselves, and only then speak.

When we get together, we usually point out, "They are Christians, these are Sikhs, those are Jews, these are Muslims." What does this mean? The prophets have not told us to say these things about each other.

Guru Gobind Singh once said, "The Provider and the Merciful One are the same. The Creator and the Bountiful One are the same. Hindu worship and Muslim prayer are the same. Temple and Mosque are the same. Understand that you are all human beings."

He said, "God has created all humans, and we should sit together as sisters and brothers. God's Love, God's Light, God's blessings are in all things. See them everywhere; love each other. Do not create these little sects and then fight over them."

We must all understand that the prophets spoke from one Light. In light, where is the fortress, where is the boundary? What is the country of light? What is the religion of light? The religion of light is love.

Throughout my life, I have been upset whenever a person takes the name of a particular religion, the name of a boundary, the name of one place. God is all-pervading. After realizing Him, look from within yourself. There is nothing outside.

Today I think we should all decide that Buddha belongs to the whole universe, that Hazrat Muhammad belongs to the whole universe, that Jesus also belongs to the whole universe, that Guru Nanak Sahib belongs to the whole universe. Then I think peace will begin from today, and violence will not continue. Why? Because there will be one Father within us all, and a great wave of love will flow throughout our family.

Share our Masters

We have made very strong fortresses within our minds. To break those fortresses we will have to use a lot of force. But if we want violence to end and peace to come to the whole world, let us today break all these forts. We are all sisters, we are all brothers. Our God is one, beneath Whom we all take birth, grow up, leave, and come again.

When you will love the whole Creation, I think Jesus will be so happy that his happiness will have no limits. Buddha will be so happy that his happiness will know no limits. Hazrat Muhammad will be so happy: "Now they are practicing my true teachings."

If somebody asks me "What is Buddha?" I will say, "Buddha is light." If somebody asks me, "What is Hazrat Muhammad Sahib?" I will say, "He is light." If somebody asks me, "What is Guru Gobind Singh?" I will say, "He is light." My mind is convinced that all of them are light. We make boundaries around them, but they are only light.

We should share our Masters. Whenever a prophet's holy day comes, we celebrate it. We don't celebrate Jesus's Birthday so that Christians will be happy, or Buddha's Birthday so that Buddhists will be happy. The only thought I have is, "These Masters are blessed by God. Take blessings from them, take healing from them. Prepare a lot of food, string lots of lights and flowers for their birthdays. Create happiness on their birthdays." Why? Because all of them are one.

I realize that I am in great need of healing and you are also in great need of healing. When we will all be healed, the wind which passes by us will also be healed, the place where our voice travels will be healed, the trees under which we sit will be healed, the very earth where we walk will be healed. Within us a fountain of healing nectar will flow, and our body will also be healed.

I will pray to God from inside, asking for His Love: "Heal all of us so that we will become such good human beings that by looking at us, others will become good. Heal all of us, and heal the whole creation." Jesus said, "In my Father's kingdom, there is great peace." May that kingdom come to earth and all of us live in peace.

I am not talking as your judge, nor as a master. I am saying only those things which all the prophets and messiahs have said. If we will not practice those things, peace will not come and violence will not disappear. When we follow their teachings, then there will be peace in the whole world. There will be no castes, no high or low. Then we will see love, love everywhere.

Mental Healing

To the International Consultation on Medical Anthropology and Alternative Systems of Healing

The greatest healing comes from looking to see what is within ourselves. We all have a wonderful power within us. Whether we are poor or rich, sinner or saint, we have light within us. The supreme truth of going deep inside oneself is that we recognize that Power which lies within us is light. When we are in love with God, kindness will develop within us, and love, and feelings of service. When our mind is healed, our thoughts will become very pure and holy, and our body will also be very happy.

By contrast, when a person is under the influence of fear, of hatred, they have a very negative effect on the body. This is our greatest ailment – that we have fear, hatred, ego, anger within us. Whenever we are under the influence of anger, every part of our body trembles. When we are afraid, fear weakens our mind and also our body. The disease of nervousness, of worry, afflicts ninety percent of people. I think that if this affliction is eradicated from the mind, all physical diseases will also end.

We may try to heal our body with the help of herbs, or allopathic medicine, or homeopathy. But who will heal our thoughts? The body may of course be healed and the ailment eliminated. But it is our thoughts which irritates us.

Everywhere people are trying to be comfortable by every means possible, be it yoga, or medicine, or acquiring big cars and big houses. But despite all this, people are not happy. We should instead transform our mind, our thoughts. When we heal our mind, disease will have very little chance to enter our body and negative thoughts will not have the opportunity to pollute our mind.

We ask how pollution can be cleansed from the world. If we see clearly, humans are the most poisonous of all creatures. When we become angry and commit a crime, a wave of poison spreads through the air. If we purify our thoughts, if we make them loving, serving, and compassionate, I think the whole world will be cleansed.

When our thoughts are poisoning us, how will worldly medicine help us? If we could achieve pleasure through medicine, then those kings who have learned doctors would be supremely happy. But both the kings and the doctors are unhappy.

The medicine for our thoughts is not worldly medicine. We can get it only from meditation. When we turn within and meet God, we will all be healed. God will heal our inner sickness and our outer sickness as well. Tens of millions of dollars being spent on medicine to cure the human body will be saved. If anger leaves us, we also will not have to spend billions on armaments. What are weapons but expressions of our anger, of our ego?

Search for the essence which lies inside everything. That same thing is lying inside me which is also inside you.

Prayer and Meditation: Healing mind, body, and society

Baba Siri Chand ji

Babaji would take time from samadhi to help us

Seated behind Guru Granth Sahib ji, during amrit ceremony at Gobind Sadan, prior to 300th anniversary of Khalsa

Garlanding Jesus in Gobind Sadan

Praying at the Muslim Shrine at Dewa Sharif, Barabanki, Lucknow

Babaji and Father Gregorios celebrate Christmas at Gobind Sadan

Singing kirtan in Mizoram–the vibrations brought peace to the strife torn area (1977)
Clockwise – IG Randhawa, Surendra Nath, M.S. Sandhu, Roshan Lal, Gov. Chhibber

Healing light from Babaji
falls on Gurcharan's father

Standing in prayer – light streaming through the darkness

In prayer at Gobind Sadan's Peace Havan *(Ralph Singh and Joginder Kaur)*

II

The Inner Life

Don't waste a moment. As soon you start meditating, reciting Nam, and seeking God's Light within yourself, your life will change.

As more and more people do so, the world will change.

Gobind Sadan's Mission

There is a Power by which we think and speak. There is nothing, throughout creation, in which this Power does not exist. But although people have little knowledge of it, this Power of God which lies within us is also in animals, in plants and flowers, in the entire cosmos.

Our programme is to help all people understand that this Power is within us and that it exists within all of Creation. When we have all understood that, we will no longer be able to hurt another's feelings, commit violent acts, deprive others of their rights, or accept the evils that we see. Why? When we look with the vision of that inner Power, we will understand that to injure another's feelings is to injure the feelings of that Power; to commit violence is to commit violence towards that Power. We will feel, understand, and see that Power which is common to all of Creation, has placed its power within the whole Creation.

After we have attained this realization, we will look at everything with the inner vision of enlightenment. We will then see that which these physical eyes cannot see. We will see that there is nothing to which we are not connected. We will see that we have a link with the mountains, the trees, the animals, the flowers, the earth, the skies, and the wind.

Why? There is one Creator who controls all of Creation. He also fills everything with His Power. He makes everything move. Yet He does not keep anything in confinement; He has made everything free. Trees grow and flourish, animals increase, rivers swell. But He is constantly overseeing everything, and He is present in everything. If He is separated from anything, it dies.

What is gyan? His Power. What is light? His Power. All things exist because He is within them. The trees whisper and animals speak, mountains rise and plants bloom on the mountains. The wind and the trees make music together, for they have become an instrument of God. Flowers give fragrance, for they have become the scent of God. God has created everything and God is moving everything. Where is God? We have to accept that God is within us.

What is the mission of Gobind Sadan? Not just to understand that Power which pervades all of Creation, but to see that Power and to attain it. But how can we attain it? By meditation, by inner love, by inner gyan, by inner compassion. To meditate is to recognize the Creator who pervades all Creation.

The prophets who have said, "Do not commit violence" did not declare it after holding meetings or debating this decision. They entered into research, so deeply that they became lost in their quest. After searching, searching, searching, they saw the Light of God within themselves. Once they saw that light inside, they immediately saw it all around them also, for that light pervades the whole cosmos. It was then that they said, "Don't commit violence. Don't cut the trees, don't kill the animals, don't kill the insects."

You must all firmly understand that there is one common force in all of Creation. It also exists in those things which we do not see, in the planetary bodies which are beyond our sight, in the stars and planets that lie beyond them, in the skies that lie beyond the beyond. But when will we be able to see that one common Power? Only when we see the gyan within us. Why? Because that Power of the cosmos is united with our inner Power, gyan. When gyan develops within us, those unseen realms will appear before us automatically, for they are connected to the light of inner wisdom.

The great thing is that when we gain this inner understanding, we will be able to understand dharam. We will understand love, we will understand service. But, it is essential to understand that Power first, for it is present in everything.

Every prophet has affirmed this. Jesus said, "Why don't you see the love of my Father everywhere? It is in flowers, in trees, in animals." Similarly, when Guru Gobind Singh looked with enlightened vision, he said, "God is in the water, God is in the earth, God is in the caves, God is in the mountains, God is here, and God is there." Likewise, the Prophet Muhammad said, "Allah is Master of the skies, Master of the earth, Master of the whole Creation." All the prophets said the same thing, after seeing Him.

When all the students, masters, and gurus of that University of Gyan came to us and said the same thing, we should pay attention to their messages. We should practice their teachings. We should act upon their teachings.

There is nothing new which you need to bring to this world. Love has already come, gyan has already come, compassion and desire to serve have already come. Scriptures have already been written. Light has come, revelation has come, truth has come, love has come. Dharam never ends. It merely needs to be remembered. When the prophet comes, by his Power, his merciful gaze, his speech and his teachings, that gyan which was hidden within a person becomes manifest. Then in what Kabir called the "storm of gyan," the person is healed, for his evils are eliminated and good comes forth.

My Childhood Experiences

To the BBC

When I was young, I use to wonder, "Why does a person die? What is it that never dies?" They say that God is eternal – that He gives birth but does not die, that He Himself remains immortal. I began to feel pulled towards Him and detached from the world. My mind would call out, "You Who do not die, where are You? What are You?" Slowly enlightenment – the inner knowledge that God exists - began to dawn within me, combined with the feeling of longing: "Where is He?" I began singing out of this awareness of His existence and crying, "What are You? Where are You?" I never searched for God in any religious institution; I had no liking for them.

One day I was sitting in our home. The buffalo were tethered there. Since God wanted to give me inner knowledge, suddenly I had a vision: "That buffalo which is standing before you will fall down and die." I was so young at the time that my beard had not yet begun to grow. The buffalo fell down dead, but what could I do? I felt shy and scared, for my father and mother were sitting there. I kept quiet. At once another vision came; "If you put your hand on the buffalo's forehead, she will come back to life." I wondered, "How can I do that? What will my father and mother think?" Then the idea came to me to put my hand on her back and ask, "What's wrong? What's wrong with you?" I put my hand on her back end and gradually rubbed it towards her head. When I reached her forehead, she jumped and sat up. Great faith filled my mind: "Achhaa (Ah hah) – the Power which killed her has also brought her to life."

We were farmers. We had no tractors, only bullocks. After a field was ploughed and seeded, we used a thick wooden plank pulled behind bullocks to cover the seed and level the soil. The men were going to level the fields, so they told me, "Bring some rope to tie the ends of the plank." I started for the field, but along the way I felt the attraction to God. So I said, "You give me the rope so that I can give it to them." As soon as this thought crossed my mind, the rope appeared on the ground in front of me. From then on, my faith increased.

One day I was walking along the muddy banks of a canal. My clothes were dirty. I said to God, "I want to wash my clothes. You do this: I need a proper place where I can wash my clothes." At once, a brick platform appeared in the water. I took off my clothes and washed them, and my faith increased even more. I said, "You assembled the bricks, You did this work for me, and that work for me, You gave life to our buffalo."

I began sitting in samadhi (spiritual absorption), asking, "Where are You who is doing all of my work?" I took off my clothes, let my hair down, and sat and sat.

Then I began to see that Power, in the form of Baba Siri Chand, Guru Nanak's elder son. Like me, he was not wearing any clothes.

After some time, Guru Gobind Singh, the Tenth Guru of Sikhs, came to me carrying clothes and shoes. He said, "Nothing comes of removing your clothes. Put on these clothes." I got up in the morning and put on the clothes. Gradually the clear vision of enlightenment increased within my mind.

In our village, a man had arranged for the continuous recitation of Guru Granth Sahib. Because this very new inner vision was increasing in me, he said, "Come to my house and offer the opening prayer." I felt very shy. What would I do there? I used to be afraid of appearing in public, and I had no knowledge of these manmade prayers.

Suddenly Guru Gobind Singh said, "Get up!" and I had a vision. I could see something like a cinema screen before my eyes. All the prophets, dervishes, Messiahs, and messengers of God passed before me, one by one. I just stood with folded hands as they each introduced themselves. I wondered, "What is this? How can I tell the public of such a great thing?" Guru Gobind Singh said, "Don't worry. I showed you this vision of all the prophets so that you will not be misguided. They are all one. Whether you speak in public or not, I wanted to teach you that religion is not for one community, or for one country, or for one group of people. The prophets all come from one Light, and they all return to the one Light. Never think that any one religion or prophet is superior to others. It is your choice whom to love, but there is no difference among them. Whomsoever you love is the Light."

Guru Gobind Singh kept telling me all these things. He said, "All religions are one. If a person praises one religion and criticizes another, don't regard that as religion. Understand that everything is one. All religions teach, "Love, speak truth, serve others, don't hurt anyone's feelings. I, too, instruct you in these ways, and all messengers of God have taught the same message."

Life's Difficult Journey

To a member of the Church of Conscious Harmony in Austin, Texas, USA

Life in this world is a great journey. If we have firm faith, love for God, a willingness to serve, and always keep God in our thoughts, even though many difficulties and obstacles arise along the way we will pass through the darkness on this endless journey. When these four things develop within you, they make such a strong base that no worldly thing can shake you from this foundation.

A person thinks that he should be able to understand all things with his own limited thoughts, and see clearly with his own limited vision. But there are certain things which are far above the realm of our comprehension. Enlightened wisdom is far beyond our worldly wisdom, for God is the Enlightenment of enlightenment. Even if we acquire enlightened knowledge, even then some of His knowledge remains hidden from us.

In the midst of worldly hardships, sometimes we ask, "I have great faith in God. Why must I suffer like this?" Listen to what I am about to tell you and accept it with love: These sufferings are a very small measure of what you were to face. You have been given a karmic shortcut. Instead of the great difficulty which was to befall you, your account has been cleared by just undergoing a small difficulty.

Many things happen that are beyond our understanding, so sometimes we are surprised, sometimes we are worried, sometimes we are afraid. We don't know whether this suffering or illness or difficult situation will be beneficial to us or not. Caught in the midst of such matters, a person is always somewhat upset.

To remain happy, look at difficulties as something great that God has done for our benefit. We do not know what the benefit is, but it is possible that there is some benefit behind our worldly difficulties. Perhaps because of these difficulties our life will become better in the future, perhaps our thoughts will become better, or perhaps we will be freed from pressure.

The Messiahs and prophets have repeated this guidance over and over again: Welcome even difficulties with love. Love God even in the midst of problems. Whatever God does, love His actions. We should be aware that nothing is outside of God. Nothing is outside of His command, His healing, His feeling, His vision. If we face any difficulties, we should have the love and faith to feel that we do not know what this difficulty really is.

The prophets and Messiahs gave us many examples to help us live in this world, to help us understand our lives. Jesus called to a dead person, and he arose. He wanted to demonstrate that God is a power so great that He can bring the dead to life, or give sight to the blind. Jesus also gave us his own example: While being crucified, he saw the crucifixion as God's love, just to show us that the nails are His love, the cross is His love, and being nailed to the cross is also His love. Without God's command, no nail, no hammer, no cross can be made, nor can people have the ability to carry out the action. This is all His power.

Sometimes a person is afraid of receiving the gifts which God sends. But never be afraid of any gift. As the Sikh Gurus have said, "Pain and hunger are always occurring. Oh Divine Giver, these are also Your gifts, for nothing is outside of You. Poverty is You, and the strength to tolerate poverty is also You. Where is it that You do not prevail?"

Even those who are the most beloved of God may be made to suffer by God. The Fifth Sikh Guru was made to sit on a hot iron plate, and hot sand was poured on him. Nonetheless, no one could destroy his love for God. He said, "I feel so happy and I dance in joy that today You have looked upon me and spoken to me." Jesus had a vision that he would be made to carry the cross, whipped, nailed to the cross, and crucified. He prayed to God, "This cup of suffering is coming. Will You not remove it?" But then suddenly, Jesus agreed, "No! This is for You. If You have earmarked this especially for me, then it is fine." God does not always send us sweet gifts. Sometimes one has to go to the gallows in His love.

At times we waver in our faith. Instead, always think that God has sent us, has given us birth, and is even more concerned about us than we are about ourselves. For example, God crafts us in a place where our first nourishment is also provided. We could not do such a thing for ourselves. When we are in our mother's womb, God knows what food to give us, how to keep us alive, by what means to shape our body's development. Even before we emerge from the womb, God is concerned about what food is to be given to us once we are born – that which will provide all nutrients, protect us from disease, and support our development. While we are still in the womb., He creates these nutrients in our mother's milk, and keeps it ready for us. It provides the best food of all for the child, the best development, the best love, the best will power. Thus we should always be aware of God's great concern for us.

Therefore try not to question what you do not understand. If we think about it, ninety per cent of things are beyond our understanding. We can only judge those things which we can see with our eyes, things which are directly before us. But we cannot see everything.

Always have faith in God and the Guru. He will always save you. Not only will He preserve your every breath in the present; He will save you in the future and He has saved you in the past. Never think that Satan will attack you. Satan will not attack any place where there is the Love and Truth of God and faith in God. There Satan will also bow before Him because Satan is also His slave. Understand that Satan is created by God and is also under His command. Satan will not do anything outside of God's command, for God's Power is Supreme. Nothing can stand against His Power.

If we look with enlightened vision, we can see that God has created everything. He has given the command for all creation only once; there has been no need for Him to issue His command a second time. The cycles He has created are continuing. By His command, everything is developing, ascending, and descending. God is so powerful that there is nothing that can go against His command.

Meditate on Your Master

How can you attain enlightenment? By focusing your mind on your master. Consider Guru Gobind Singh or Guru Nanak, for instance. They can assume all forms. Look at the trees: It is they who bestow light upon them. Look at animals: It is they who are giving them life. But when we sit in meditation, in order to concentrate, we have to focus our minds on one who has brought the message of God and is joined with God. Then we will begin to feel something arise within us. We will see that Power all around us and also inside us.

Actually, the enlightenment of meditation is within us. But when we sit in meditation, it is essential to focus on the master whose teachings or actions are most appealing to us. Understand this well: The light of all the masters is the same, their qualifications are the same, the Word is the same. But you must choose one. Perhaps Guru Nanak is most appealing to you, for you like his way of speaking, his politeness, his way of teaching. Or perhaps you feel that what Guru Gobind Singh, or Jesus, or Moses said was right. Actually, what all the prophets said is right. But you will have to choose one and concentrate upon that one.

When you sit in meditation, concentrate upon the master you choose. In this way, your scattered thoughts will focus in one place. When your mind is focused, what will happen? As Kabir said, "My mind has become pure like the water of the Ganges. What I used to see in the outer world, now I can see inwardly."

Furthermore, Kabir said, "An amazing thing has happened. With meditation, my identity has vanished, and now when I say, 'Ram, Ram,' Ram is following me saying, 'Kabir, Kabir.' I questioned Him: 'I am the one to be blessed, You are the Giver of Blessings.' Ram replied, 'Ram and Kabir have become one. Your personal identity is no more; the name your mother gave you is no more. Now you have become Brahmgyani (enlightened one).' "

There is no issue of idolatry. We learn everything from form. Guru Nanak came into the world with the same hands and feet like us in order to teach us about enlightenment. Guru Gobind Singh came and spoke like us, so we could learn about enlightened wisdom. When Brahma (a form of God) came and spoke, the Vedas (India's ancient scriptures) were created for our understanding.

Those who came to us possessed great powers. The head of Baba Deep Singh was severed, yet holding it in one hand, he wielded a sword with his other hand in order to reach the threshold of the Golden Temple and place his head before his Guru, as he had vowed. As Guru Gobind Singh says, "The One Light pervades the heavens and earth. It neither increases nor decreases." In Baba Deep Singh that power had manifested which cannot be severed, cannot be decreased, cannot be torn, cannot be pierced with an arrow. His head of flesh was severed, but he had attained that inner strength of enlightenment which can never be severed.

Concentration of the mind

In order to meditate, sit in a comfortable position, as long as you can, with your body relaxed. With great love, concentrate on the master whom you have chosen. Keep sitting for some time. You may feel your mind wandering. Then slowly, slowly, slowly, the mind begins to become steady. When that concentration is achieved, the mind does not waver.

The average person's thoughts are scattered in many directions. "What will happen at work?" "What will happen to my children?" "What will happen to my wife?" "What will happen after my retirement?" "Will my boss be good or not? What will my boss do?"

When you concentrate on the master, your mind will remain focused. Then you will say to God, as Guru Gobind Singh did in Jaap Sahib, "You are the Cause of all actions. You will do all my work. You are the Benevolent Provider of my sustenance."

Your concentration will slowly, slowly increase. A child tears his primer in the first class, but as he gradually learns, he tells his mother, 'Please bind my book; please give it a cover'. We ourselves are children. When enlightened wisdom begins to manifest in us, we will see His form in everyone. We will see His form in the whole cosmos. We will look upon everyone with mercy.

The greatest thing in meditation is utter quietness. The difference between meditation and prayer or worship is that as we worship or pray, we say something, whereas to meditate is to turn inside, think of the Guru, and listen to what he says. To begin, gently turn your attention toward your Guru. If your master is Guru Nanak, you might think of how Guru Nanak sat in contemplation, how he spoke, how he became one with God. Think of that Light which fell upon him: What was its color? He brought healing everywhere – he healed the air, he healed the trees. Focus your mind on these scenes. Then those qualities which you are concentrating on will begin to develop within you.

If you like Guru Gobind Singh, concentrate on him. He has no form; yet he creates myriad forms. As he said to God, " You are ever manifest in all Your splendor, ever present in all Thy glory." After coming into the world, Guru Gobind Singh said, "I was deep in meditation on the timeless and mighty God who transcends death. Neither time nor weather have any effect on Him, for He is eternal. My attention was deeply fixed upon His feet." Guru Gobind Singh himself focused his attention on an image.

Keep the object of your concentration in your mind always, not only when you sit in meditation but even when you sit in your office, so that you form the habit. When you focus on that Power when meditating, it will begin to develop inside you. When you are sitting in your office, think of Him. When food comes before you, think of Him. When tea is before you, think of Him. Always think, "Oh Maharaj, this is Your gift. Please be gracious." Then you will feel that He is in everything.

Guru Gobind Singh and Guru Nanak were not ordinary people; they were sent by God. The form of these powers is omnipresent. But you must develop some specific image and focus on that. Thus you will attain success. Slowly, slowly your mind will begin concentrating, and then you will turn within.

Communion with God

When the mind turns within, you will reach the state that Kabir described, "You are me and I am You; there is no difference." Then you will continually talk with Him within yourself and all around you. The masters have given these instructions to us. Always keep them in mind. If we have come to know anything about God, about Creation, about the path, we have learned it from the masters. Guru Nanak Sahib came to the world and said, "God is the Master of the whole Creation." The Prophet Muhammad came and said, "He is Master of the Heavens and Master of the Earth. He has no equal; He is the only One. Fight the great battle to control your mind, and commune with Him." Jesus said, "Love my Father. My Father is the only One." "He called God his Father, and so did Guru Gobind Singh. Guru Gobind Singh said, God spoke to me: 'Go – I appoint you My son. I give all My boons to you, all My powers to you.' Whatever He told me, I am repeating to you. I cannot remain silent in this transient world. I have come to deliver God's message."

Become so joined with God that you feel Him wherever you are. Develop a relationship with Him. The Fifth Guru says, "You are my Mother, You are my Father, You are my Relative, You are my Brother." He said, "Develop any kind of relationship with Him. There is no other Relative in the world like God." Guru Nanak says to God, "You are my Friend, You are my dearest Girlfriend."

God is very powerful. He is the Master of Creation, the Master of the Cosmos. He is our Master also. He is the One Who runs our brain, Who does justice from within us, Who gives us wisdom from within, Who reminds us of the good of society. He is very merciful. He gives us work. He gives us the ability to sleep. To some He gives cars, servants, families. Why shouldn't we stay focused on Him? Guru Ram Das says, "He takes care of our every breath. How can we not be thankful to Him?"

God is not in a walled fortress; God is sitting within us giving us His life. As the Fifth Guru said, "Where does God live? He is sitting on the tongue of saints". When a person meditates, God remains on his tongue twenty-four hours a day. He is not confined to some building. As Saint Ravidas says, "He is sitting within you, nearer than your hands and feet." Your hands and feet are farther from you than God.

It is essential that we meditate, for meditation clears the effects of our thoughts and actions. When we meditate, our karmas are burned and our inner enlightenment is illuminated. Kabir said, "The storm of enlightenment has come, and ignorance has gone, I know not where."

Therefore, you must turn your attention toward the guru and meditate as much as you can. But the twenty-four-hour-a-day meditation is this: When you grasp a pen, think of God. Think of Him as you sit in your office. Whenever you do something, always think of Him: "Oh God, all this is Yours. I am nothing. People come and stand at my door because of Your blessing. I am Your servant, for You have chosen me, and I must serve You."

Give your life

You will not attain enlightenment just by closing your eyes. If your mind is still scattered, worrying, you will be in the same position after closing your eyes as before. To advance in any endeavour, you must give your life to the effort. A village person cannot learn to use a stethoscope just by holding it in his hand. To become a doctor, one must persevere and study for 25 to 30 years. Telephones were not created by mere talk; scientists have devoted their entire lives so we might sit under the electric light, watch television, and speak to people just by picking up a phone.

Similarly, you can only become enlightened by giving your life to the effort. Kabir said, "Only that person can pass Ram's test who has become dead in life." Ask gold how it has come to adorn a lady's ear. It will say, "Ask the goldsmith. I was just a lump. He put me in the furnace so that none of my identity remained. I became a fiery coal. I was annihilated. Then he moulded me. Because I was completely transformed, now I have become a lady's fine earrings, a necklace for a queen, and sit beneath a canopy over the head of a king."

When does a jewel become precious? When it is cut into a proper shape. The more it is cut, the greater its value. When a diamond is cut by a master diamond-cutter, its light is revealed. Wood is of no great value until it meets the master carver. Then it becomes a throne for a king or queen. The Five Beloveds of Guru Gobind Singh offered their heads, and thus they rose so high that the Guru himself sat inside them. The Guru is a diamond cutter. His arrows carve away our evils, revealing our inner light.

Mind and Soul

To devotees from Moscow

There are two things: One we call mind – our thoughts, our nature. Our mind is affected by all the impressions from this life and previous lives, impressions from our parents, traits inherited from our ancestors, and the impressions of our environment. The second thing is what we call atma. It is above all these influences. The atma is that which keeps us alive and which gives us consciousness and enlightenment. All religions speak of this eternal aspect in a human being, though they give it different names, such as "ruh," "soul," "atma," "fravashi," or "Buddha-nature."

What happens when we sit in meditation? If a musical instrument is lying untouched, it will not make any sound. But when one strokes a finger across the strings, then it begins to emit sounds.

Similarly, when shabd (God's Holy Name) is coupled with surat (attention) they touch and awaken our atma. As shabd and surat strike each other – like two stones struck together to kindle a fire – the enlightened consciousness of our atma becomes illuminated.

Once we reach that state, our nature will continue to exist, but it will no longer trouble us, for when a bright light appears, a dim light disappears. That dim light of our karmas will pack its bags and leave, and our troubling thoughts will cease. The light of the atma remains. It was this light to which the Guru referred when he said, "When that Light was kindled in your body, you took birth in the world." In the fourth state (the highest state of spiritual development) what remains is the eternal atma. It cannot be burned, drowned, or cut.

The Guru says, "This atma comes from another realm, and the clothes it wore have caught fire from all sides." At death, the body is burned, but the atma is untouched. The effects of the person's actions also remain, determining his next birth. What will happen when he is reborn? His karmas will rejoin his atma in the womb of his new mother, and thus the two will remain together.

The inward path

The karmas attached to your mind keep us wavering. They create fear, worry, and greed. We must find a path through them. We may call it illumination of the atma, or opening of the Third Eye, or awakening of our intuition. When you turn inside, focusing your eyes on that path rather than on your thoughts, what will happen? When that small light joins the great Light, then those troubling thoughts will loosen their grip. Their power will weakened, like an enemy who thinks twice before attacking again.

The karmas which beset the mind are not permanently attached to the atma. When Kabir attained enlightenment, he said, "Ram (God) and Kabir have become one. My nature and habits have ended, my mind has disappeared. Only the infinite atma remains. Ram is looking at me and I am looking at Him."

The saint Nam Dev was asked, "What is God like?" He replied, "Look at your face in the water. God is like the face that you see in the water." He could only say this when his mind was defeated and his atma was illumined. He said to God, "You are me, I am You. There is no difference between us." In this state, whatever God is, you are, for the atma has merged with the Great Atma. Nam Dev said, "It is infinite, infinite."

You might understand the mind and atma in this way: A king is sitting on a throne. Many armies are working under him, but not everyone can see him. He is giving the orders, but those who carry out the orders are separate.

Or think of it like this: There is a bulb inside us which is illuminated and giving light, but there is a cover over it. Mosquitoes and other bugs will land on the cover and affect it, but the bulb is safe inside. That light of consciousness itself is dharam. When it's illuminated your self-existence disappears and His existence takes its place.

Nam Dev was a human being. But he turned away from his thoughts and actions and focused on the Master. There were enemies on every side, ahead and behind, but he passed through them and communicated directly with his Master.

Faith and Love

To volunteers from Gobind Sadan, USA

Why do we revere the Messiah, the prophets? We may say that God is very great, very powerful, but the prophets know that this is true. They know that nothing transpires without their Father's order. They had so much faith that by their very word or glance even a cripple was healed. They knew that nothing was too great for God to do, that even a dead body could be raised again. These thoughts do not occur in an ordinary person. He says, "How could that possibly happen?" The Messiah says, "All things are possible."

There is another quality which distinguishes prophets from ordinary people: They gladly take on the problems of others. We become annoyed if we have to take on even a little of another's problems.

Therefore, it is not only we humans who are worshipping the One whom we call God, and those whom we call Messiah or Prophet. Their deeds are so great that the air, the trees, and the water are worshipping them and the ground is kissing them, even though we cannot see it. Their sacrifice, their love, and their faith are so great that the entire cosmos is bowing to them. We cannot see the flowers saying, "What beautiful colours God has given us," but they are telling Him. Thus the prophet says, "Look at the flowers. Then you will see how beneficent my Father is."

The person who has both faith and love has no equal in the world. Why? Until one has faith, how can one serve humanity? Until one has love, how can one serve? Service comes later; faith and love are the prerequisites for which there is no substitute.

Love is that in which there are no demands. If there is any demand, then it is not love. Faith is that in which if someone says, "How is it possible?" one asserts, "It is possible." If there is the slightest doubt, then faith is not complete. Love and faith were fully present in the Messiah, in the Prophets, so healings occurred, they would screen all people's problems with their vision, and blessings fell like rain.

Sometimes we worry, and yet we claim to have faith. If you have faith, why are you worried? We say we have full faith, but sometimes we are afraid. If you have faith, how can you even think of fear? In faith, your thoughts are fully attached to the One you love. When you are in love, nothing else can enter your consciousness. When a person falls in love, he is thinking of his beloved twenty-four hours a day. Nothing else in the world appeals to him except his beloved. When one loves God, there is nothing else like Him. Love therefore has no eyes, no tongue, no ears; love is unique unto itself. Love itself listens, speaks, and guides us, for there is nothing present but love.

Try to set your self aside and let your mind move forward toward God. Once you are connected with God, there will be no words you can use to express that feeling. No one has yet been able to describe that taste, that desire which comes when we are in love with God. We cannot even create a thought about it, so how could we express it? If a thought to express that love comes into your mind, you will immediately regret it, feeling, "No – it is so much greater than that!" At last we will just give up and sit silently, feeling, "There is nothing I can say to describe You."

The combination of love and faith has been held in high esteem from the beginning of time. The prophets and Messiahs met hundreds of thousands of people, but this combination was not present in many. Jesus called the one in whom both were present "Peter" (the Rock). The prophet heals millions of people, but he gives responsibility only to a few. He chooses those with love and faith, and then says to them, "Go carry on this work." Wherever these people whom the prophet had chosen went, whatever they said automatically healed people. Until we are healed, the bad things within our inner storeroom cannot be removed.

Never count your years. Look at the Spirit within you, which is ageless. It is light. The Light never becomes older or younger. Its lifetime is unlimited. It is always childlike in its innocence, and its love. Those who have been God's people have always showered their blessings, never thinking how or upon whom the blessings are falling. Just as a child will go to anyone who comes and say, "Pick me up," a person is drawn to God to say, "Take me." Just so, the Messiah always reaches out, takes our sins, lifts them up, and cleanses them. Those who are one with God often say, "Love children;" for they themselves are like children. They are innocently healing people all the time, with no knowledge, just as a child is always innocently reaching out in love.

Always keep love and faith firmly connected. They will attempt to separate, but follow them and keep them together, as if you were shepherding children. When these two are united, an aura will form around you such that wherever you look, you will no longer see anyone's bad qualities or good qualities. You will see only that Light.

Although we are all praying, each in our own ways, healing is not occurring, for we have separated love and faith from our prayers. We have forgotten the most important thing: to concentrate upon healing ourselves. Most people are slipping twenty-four hours a day because they are standing on the uncertainty of their own ego and their own anger. Until we remove the greed, the anger, and the ego from within ourselves, how can we help or heal anyone else?

Every day we pray and ask for God's order, and yet we pull our heads away from God's blessing. The light is falling, but we do not stay beneath it. When we allow God's Light to come within us and heal us, the effect of that inner healing will touch other people. Faith and love are always within us, and the One who heals is always within us.

How to Develop Faith?

To a journalist from the United States

There are two forms of faith. The first is the inner attraction toward God and detachment from the world. The second form of faith is based on actually observing something happen.

As a person sits in meditation, concentrating on some manifestation of God, this focus becomes translated into actual events. The more one sees the practical actions of God, the more one's faith develops.

If a person witnesses something which is unexpected, beyond logic, his faith increases. For example, Jesus went among some people who were against him. Among them was a blind beggar.

He called out to Jesus, so the Lord restored his sight. Previously he had no faith that Jesus could restore his sight or that Jesus was the Messiah. But when he and the other people witnessed this event, they developed faith that this Doctor could perform "x-rays" and "operations" and bestow light.

If you stay at Gobind Sadan, every day you will see things happen here which are beyond reason. Then your faith will increase. Or perhaps your friends will feel an inner happiness, love, fearlessness within you, and on feeling it, will ask, "Why are you different from us?" You will answer, "I simply pray." As you do, your weaknesses will gradually disappear and faith will develop within you.

If we really try to determine what faith is, we must conclude that it is a matter of divine blessing. In the time of Jesus, miracles occurred daily. But the day came when the faith of all of his followers was broken. This proves that faith does not result from seeing miracles. Faith is a matter of blessing. If you are not blessed, you will not have faith even after seeing miracles. If a saint says to a person, "Go! You will remain linked with God," that person cannot break off from God. His faith will remain constant, whether or not he sees miracles.

Faith is an intangible inner quality. Within us there develops an inexplicable feeling of love, of divine wisdom, of desire to serve. What is it which prompts you to serve the blind? Which prompts you to be with lepers, with the crippled? What is it that makes you happy when you are among such people? Other people will not go near them. The one who goes to them does not know why she goes, nor does another know why he does not go. If you ask that person why she stands among such people, she will simply answer, 'I just like to do so.'

Faith and love cannot be measured

When the saint sits in meditation, day after day, he or she experiences the existence of God, the truth of God, and the power of God, and describes the experiences for the people. It is not that the saint has great faith. Rather, God is happy with the saint, so God keeps showing the saint these things which God does not reveal to others.

The main point is that love is in God's hands. It has no form, so one cannot say how it is created. It has no dress, no voice, so how could it be created? It has no language – what language does love speak?

Many powerful Messiahs, prophets, and saints have appeared in all countries. The best thing to do is to concentrate on whichever one you prefer. At first, concentrate even without faith. If faith were within people's control, we would all become Jesus, we would all become Moses. Why don't we? Because only the one whom God chooses develops faith. Nevertheless, you must pray and try to develop an attitude of service and love within yourself. Some other Power is behind all this, but keep trying. Perhaps some day you will be able to experience that path of Light, that path of Love.

There is a Controller Who is running everything. Only a person who understands this can speak about or see that Power. Others are doubtful. The difference is quite distinct. One mother says, "Jesus has taken my child. Why should I be upset?" Another mother cries, "Why has the Lord taken my child? I go to church every day." Actually, the only person who has faith is the one who says, "My child has gone to Jesus. Why should I be disturbed?"

When there is bargaining in love, always be skeptical that it is actually love. Love is that in which there are no demands. One who loves says, "Even if you are angry with me, I am still yours. If you take away my home, I am still yours. If you cause a fight in my family, I am still yours. Even if there is sickness, I am still yours." Such a person is blessed by God. No matter what happens, she is still happy regardless.

What is the proof of love? That it is never measured. The greater the sacrifice, the greater the love. People who loved have been crucified, fed to lions; their houses were burned, their families were killed. But even then they kept praising God. On the cross itself, Jesus said, "Forgive and bless those who are crucifying me, who are mocking me." His love made the people realize that God loves us. Even if we are being crucified, it is God's love that we are receiving.

Many difficulties come in the path of our love for God. You might think you love a person but if he does something you do not like, you will feel aggrieved. However, if you really love that person, you give up any expectations. Whatever he does, you accept.

One who truly loves God is not aware of himself. If love is conscious, it is not love. They cut off the hands of Mansur, and yet he did not notice. He kept saying, "An al-Haqq – I am the Truth," for he was immersed in his Beloved, and who can cut off the hands of Allah? Who can tear off the skin of Allah? The lover does not even know what is happening to him. A cup of poison was given to Mirabai (the great devotee of Lord Krishna). She saw her beloved Lord Krishna in the person carrying the cup, so she drank it as nectar and sang to her Lord.

Love has no consciousness, no eyes, no legs, no thought. No one can know what love is. If love had eyes, how could one be hung on the cross? If love had legs, how could one walk toward the cross? The lovers of God did not even feel what was happening to them. They did not cry out, for they had given their whole mind to their Beloved. Pain is perceived by the mind, but their mind had been taken by Someone Else. As the Guru says, "The servant's love remains constant to the last." Faith and love are therefore inner matters. And I will say to you, they depend on God's blessings.

Why Aren't We Enlightened?

Celebration of Guru Nanak's Birthday at the home the late Dr.Bhai Mohan Singh, Former Chairman of Ranbaxy, Ltd

We bow daily before Guru Granth Sahib and listen to the words of the Gurus being read. But why is there no change in us? While we take daily guidance from scripture, our inner vices still have not left us.

When Nam enters us, ignorance leaves. When the Gurus' orders enter our consciousness, our ignorance departs. We are outwardly bowing before Guru Nanak, but he says, "Speak truth. Do not tell lies. In Nanak's house there is only Nam." What is that Nam? It is the Light. It is enlightened wisdom. It is the splendour of God. It is the secret conversation between Guru Nanak and God. When you recite Nam, it is as if millions of suns are illuminated.

We say that we recite Nam and that we have faith in Guru Granth Sahib. If so, is there any room for lies? For sins? For anger? If we imbibe Nam and the Gurus' enlightened words, anger, sins and greed all depart. If we ask You for some material gift, it only brings pain and sorrow. Oh Grantor of contentment, please give us Nam so that the hunger of our hearts will be satisfied." Guru Nanak stressed Nam again and again. He said "In Kali Yuga only Nam will save you." If we recite Nam our sins will be burned away and enlightenment will arise within us.

When a person goes to school every day and yet shows no improvement, is the weakness in the person or in the school? Is it that the Guru does not want us to improve or that we do not want to follow? Otherwise, in every school a person is transformed. When even a small child goes to school he starts speaking English, starts reading primers. But in God's school, we do not even know what the lesson is each day.

Someone who goes to a film, will later sing the film tunes as he rides along on his bicycle. But we forget the daily lesson from scripture as soon as we leave the gate of the gurdwara. This means that we are less interested in the divine message than a cinema-goer is interested in a movie.

There are many Names of God

From time immemorial, people have been chanting "Sohang, Sohang," "Ram, Ram," "Narain, Narain," "Gobind, Gobind," "Hari, Hari," "Allah, Allah" and all such Names are incorporated in Guru Granth Sahib. We have been trying to build a fort around Guru Granth Sahib, but it cannot be walled up, for. it not only contains all religions, but also the One from which all religions have come. God Himself is present in it. Now what has happened is that we have made separate religions out of different shabds (Names of God). We have turned the different names of God into separate religions. This causes clashes, with each person saying, "My religion is best." But there is no truth in this, for Wahe Guru is not exclusively Sikh, nor is Narain Hindu, nor is Allah Muslim. These Names are matters of spiritual experience.

When an enlightened being saw in vision that primeval condition in which water covered the earth, he exclaimed, "Narain, Narain" – "You are the One Who prevails throughout the waters." Another saw God as Gobind, "The One who gives light in the darkness." Another said, "Wah, Wah!," which means "Wondrous! You are so Wondrous that Your colour, form, caste, community, or country cannot be described." Sikhs may say, "Wahe Guru is our Name for God," but it is a Name belonging to all of creation. It is the shabd of the animals, the trees, the oceans, for God's wonder is in all Creation.

When we praise one prophet but criticize others, God's happiness disappears. In Guru Granth Sahib, the Gurus speak of Lord Rama, of Lord Krishna, of Allah. Why? Because there were no barriers in their hearts. From where Guru Nanak spoke, there was only light, light, light. He never created any boundaries. On the contrary, he broke the boundaries that people had created, and he stood by Nam alone.

We have not attained enlightenment because we have emphasized things which the prophets did not say. When you stress things that people have said, one person will say one thing, and another will say something else, and a third will say something else. Then there will be a clash of ideas. When we will speak only of the Teachers' words, then there will be no hatred among us. The darkness in our hearts will vanish.

Our Hidden Record

All our desires are attached to our soul. Our soul is never destroyed; it lives on for hundreds of thousands of years. Even though you will leave the body some day, your soul will take birth again. You will have the same habits and nature, and the same things which pleased you here will please you in the next life.

Sometimes a person makes a mistake without knowing it; this brings a great loss in the future. There is a kind of wireless transmitter within you, as it were, and everything is being recorded, twenty-four hours a day. The Prophet Muhammad explained that angels are always beside us, recording our account. How many times have we become angry? How many times have we doubted God? How many times have we loved God from within? Everything is being clearly recorded, even while we are sleeping at night.

This process which God has hidden from us is very dangerous, for you take birth with that record. In God's court, there is no need for witnesses or questioning the record. The one who writes the record is incorruptible; he gives a clean and straightforward report. If people became aware of this report, corruption would end, crime would end, stealing would end, loss of character would end. But people do not know, for the recording goes on invisibly.

You may be sitting innocently; anger arises within. The Ninth Guru warned us, "Beware of unconscious sin." You may not recognize that inner anger, but he cautioned us to beware even of those subconscious feelings which arise by themselves from within, for they, too, are recorded.

As long as you do not see that Power next to you, you will make mistakes twenty-four hours a day. If you think, "It doesn't matter. I'll do this thing, for I will gain, even though somebody else will lose," this is very bad for your future. He is Light, Justice, the Master of the whole Creation. He has His own ways of taking away whatever you have gained by wrongful means.

There is a story: Someone's shoe was torn. He took it to a cobbler, who stitched it together with a bit of leather, in village fashion. As soon as the shoe was fixed, its owner said, "I have no money to pay for the repair." The cobbler observed, "I've heard you have great faith in the Guru." The shoe owner piously replied, "Everything is the Guru's." The cobbler said, "Never mind then. Pay me whenever you can." The other man then forgot about that little leather patch, and never paid the money.

In a later birth, the cobbler became a falcon and the man with the shoe a partridge. Guru Gobind Singh held both of them, one in each hand, and then set them to fight. His disciples protested, "Maharaj, the partridge is in great pain." The Guru replied, "He has mortgaged a small piece of flesh in the Guru's name. I am just repaying my debt. I must pay it back, because he pledged it in my name."

When a person has great love for God, God never lets him go astray. The person who has neither love nor faith in God is a wanderer. His conscience is dead. He is like a stray dog, not a trained dog with a collar. Even so, God has His own ways of leading him to the right path.

A stricter standard

God's blessings are available to all, but they are taken only by the person who has faith and love for God. Along with the blessings, the disciple also accepts the Guru's corrections. To him, the Master says only a few words: "Why did you do that?" or "Why did you commit corruption?"

It is said that one day as Guru Nanak was passing the house of his disciple Moola, he said, "Call Moola. We have not met for a long time." Moola thought that Guru Nanak had come to take him away on his long travels, so he told his wife to tell the Guru that he was not at home. So she said to Guru Nanak, "It is our good fortune that you are calling him, but Moola is not at home."

Guru Nanak laughed heartily and said, "She has said, 'He is not here.' So be it. He is not here." The Guru left and within two minutes, Moola was dead.

Moola's wife ran after Guru Nanak, begging for his help. The Guru said, "Why did you tell a lie? Now this statement – 'He is not here' – has come from my tongue, and God will not interfere with that. But don't cry. God is very merciful, very forgiving. In the garb of the Tenth Guru, I will forgive him."

If Moola had not had a loving relationship with the Guru, the Guru would not have gone to his house. But the words had already come from his mouth, and whatever a dervish says comes to pass. God does not interfere with the dervish's word, for God himself has spoken from their tongue.

Several hundred years later, Guru Gobind Singh was hunting. Moola had taken birth as a rabbit. Perhaps the Guru went to the place where he was living just for his sake. As it is written in Gurbani. "The Creator's ways are known to Him alone." Only God knows what the Guru knows. When he reached that place, where there is now a famous gurdwara, Guru Gobind Singh shot the rabbit with an arrow, saying, "Now go. You are liberated."

The nawab (local ruler) who was hunting with him asked the Guru why he always uttered such words when shooting his arrows. Maharaj said, "I have not come to hunt. People who have committed sins in the past have come back as animals and I have come to forgive them." The nawab was skeptical. "How can we know who that rabbit was previously?" Maharaj said, "I was looking at his former life." Then he showed the nawab the scene in which Moola had lied. When the vision passed, the nawab pleaded before the Guru with folded hands, "I myself have had many tensions and difficulties because of my mistakes. Please forgive me."

Look what a punishment you must get for one lie. And a person tells thousands of lies. Even when a person becomes irritated, that is recorded. The one who keeps the records is sitting there twenty-four hours a day with his wireless receiver, calculating the accounts of the entire Creation. His computer is never wrong.

Here you can tamper with a meter, but there is no way of pushing his meter forward or back.

It is very strange that God has kept this matter secret. But those who have meditated have seen it. Jesus, Moses, the Prophet Muhammad, and Guru Nanak revealed that there are always angels with us, watching and recording everything.

Therefore, control your thoughts. Why meditate? In order to control your thoughts. With meditation, our inner divine knowledge manifests, and our ignorance is suppressed.

Our conscience dies; the prophet appears

We may think we are doing something secretly, but what secret can you conceal? Our every breath is counted, our life force is measured, our thoughts are written. From whom can you hide? God is in every particle, in every pore of our body.

We may make some mistake, such as lying or usurping someone's rights. From within, our conscience speaks for a second – "This is not correct" – but we keep doing it. It is like a father who says, "Son, liquor is bad," but even after ten years of repeating it, the son still comes home drunk. The father feels like a fool. "I've been saying this for ten years. What's the use? It's just a waste of time."

In the same way, inside every person there is a conscience explaining to him what is wrong. You may call it the light of God, or the power of God. It says to you, "Don't do this. This is a bad thing." Eventually, our conscience says, "What can I do? He doesn't listen to me." It gives up trying, saying, "I'm nothing. You are free to do as you like."

When the conscience of the whole world is dead, then God comes in bodily form, with hands and feet and tongue. The conscience has appealed to God, saying, "Nobody is listening to me now." God replies, "You reconcile your accounts. Now I will take birth, with hands and feet." It is at that time that the prophet or dervish (saint) appears. Then the question of the inner conscience does not arise, for that Voice of God sits squarely before a person, saying to him, "When I told you not to do that, why did you do it?" Then the people abandon their wrong actions and are healed.

You may be bow your head at some holy place, but there is nothing that prohibits you from stealing, for your conscience has died. You have removed the Master from your mind, even though the Master is not removable. You do not even know that the Master is there. If you saw the Ninth Guru sitting there with crossed legs when you bow your head at Sis Ganj gurdwara, you would be unable to face him. You would throw yourself on the ground before him with your eyes closed.

God appears in bodily form when many people have become debased. Why would He come otherwise? God is ever present, existing from time immemorial. God's existence never ends. God is indestructible.

This is why we celebrate the birthdays of the prophets. We thank God because that day when our conscience was dead, He sent a person like us to make it strong again, to awaken our hidden inner wisdom, to clean what had become dirty. We say to God, "Our conscience was dead, but You sent a person like us to stand before us with Your Power. You are eternal, but we didn't know about the Eternal. The Master came before us and spoke, and thus we came to know. He came with that inner Power that would transform us. When he spoke, divine knowledge was born within us."

Our Troubles Are God's Gifts

To a founding member of the Peace College in Berlin

Whatever difficulty, or love, or suffering attracts you toward God, we should understand that this is God's way of giving you a gift. When God put into your mind the idea that when you were run over by a truck your guardian angel came to save you, that moment and that idea were filled with good fortune which will benefit you for your entire life.

As it is written in Guru Granth Sahib, "Suffering is the remedy, pleasure is the disease." That time of trouble worked upon you like a curative medicine. Your faith is very strong. It will triumph and you will start walking again. Your love was great, for it was not shaken during that difficult time.

True love is proven only when a person is passing through a period of struggle. Jesus always had great love overflowing in him. But after his crucifixion the whole world came to know that he had no enemy. He was a friend to foes as well as to his friends. The message spread throughout the world that Jesus forever befriended and blessed those who nailed him to the cross and taunted him.

During your suffering, that binding chain of love remains intact within you. These are the ways of God, God's ways of teaching and training us. Undoubtedly, the intense trials which the world is now undergoing may bring a good result. Perhaps God has chosen this way to send His love into the world.

Sometimes a person might think, "If I had a good car, I would not be worried. If I had a good house, I might not be worried. If I had good food to eat, I would not be worried. If I had a good job or a powerful position, I might attain joy." God gave good food, good home, good livelihood, and physical strength, yet the person's mind was not happy. So God has thoughtfully chosen a good way to show him, "You never ask for that Joy which brings joy, that Peace which brings peace."

Perhaps now all are hungry, all want happiness. Perhaps when one is in need and then receives what he needs, he appreciates it. Now we long for God to give us love, joy, peace, and His contentment. Perhaps now we will be thankful to Him for the riches He has given to us, and we will respect Him. There is nothing beyond God's control. It is my faith that when He wants it to happen, everything will be transformed into love, faith and service.

This period will not remain as stressful as it is now. Even our worldly father, on seeing our difficulties, will try to ward them off from his child with whatever strength and love he has. But our loving and merciful spiritual Father will take us above all difficulties, because we are all His family, His children. Whether we are worthy or not, He knows, "They are Mine." He will surely clasp His children to His breast.

With Meditation, God Gives Us His Qualities

When a person meditates in his love for God, God gives His qualities to the person –qualities that are hidden within us, such as truth, compassion, willingness to serve, and love. The greatest thing that God gives is the awareness of Himself, the One who gives light to all of His Creation. When this awareness comes, then the person feels from his heart, as Gurbani says, "I see no one as an enemy or a stranger. I get along with everyone." Then the person feels God's Light, God's Love, and God's Truth everywhere, and communicates with Him.

There are great blessings and power in practicing meditation. Through meditation the Nami (God) is perceived through recitation of His Nam. Both good and bad qualities are stored within each person. When a person recites Nam, a whirlwind of gyan comes, and nothing remains but His Light. When we meditate, the door to the good qualities stored inside us opens. When we do bad acts, the door to our bad qualities opens. We should knock at the door of good qualities, and perhaps the other door will remain closed.

With every breath, we should thank God and take His Name. Thus a person becomes boundless, both here and above.

God does not give us power so that we can put pressure on others. God empowers us to deal properly and justly with others. The best policy for us is to never do toward others that which we ourselves do not like. We do not like anger, criticism, jealousy, or deprivation of our rights – why should we give them to others? Whatever you give to others, will return to you.

Meditation is essential to take God's virtues and good feelings from our inner storehouse. Religion is a school of the mind which teaches us to leave our evils and believe in goodness.

The story is told of Guru Nanak that someone once asked him how to remain always happy. He replied, "Love God and be happy when you see someone of higher status than you, be friendly to those of equal status as you, and be compassionate toward those of lower status than you. Then you will remain happy forever."

The ego is always in conflict with Nam. As Gurbani says, "Nam is opposed to the ego. They can never reside together." Love God while you work and while you serve people. Never say "I." Always say "You." You will still do the work, but you will not be discouraged with the results, because you are remembering God all the time, working hard, and depending on Him for all things.

Those people are always blessed who love God, who have compassion for others in their hearts, and who want to see others always happy. God is happy with those who love Him and who love His creations.

III

Suffer the Little Children to Come Unto Me

If children go astray, it is not their fault; it is their parents' fault.

Preventing Child Neglect and Divorce

Statement for a group working in California to help prevent child neglect and abuse

There are two essential things to be done from earliest infancy: As soon as the umbilical cord is cut, the mother should clasp the child to her heart, and nurse the baby with her own milk. From then on, the mother will feel affection toward the child, and the child toward the mother. The mother will never forsake the child, nor the child the mother. These are natural ways of love which should be carefully nurtured. Scientists and doctors confirm that they automatically create a bond between the mother and child.

Look at animals. If you take away a mother cow, she will cry for her calf and try to run toward it time and time again. The calf will also cry, "Where has my mother gone?" Why? Because the calf drinks its mother's milk, and when the calf is born, the mother licks it naturally. In our holy scripture, Guru Granth Sahib, it is written that even if the mother cow has been taken to graze on lush vegetation five miles away from her calf, she will cry, "Where is my child? I am eating, but I don't know how my child is." Her thoughts are with her calf, because the calf drinks her milk.

We humans have broken this bond of natural affection. In the name of "advanced" we have turned to feeding babies milk in bottles. Unless the mother gives her own milk to the child and embraces the child, child neglect will persist.

In addition, parents should give time to the child, for a child requires their love. If mothers and fathers spend time with their children, perhaps the children will stop using drugs. They are taking drugs because they feel lonely. There is no one to speak with them or listen to them. When they miss that support from their parents, where else will they seek it? In drugs. If children go astray, it is not their fault; it is their parents' fault.

Now there are many broken homes, but children need both parents. When there is a divorce, the child is once orphaned. One parent says, "I will take the child," while the other says, "No, I will take the child." But nobody cares for the feelings of the child who is caught in the middle. If one of the parents takes him, he still wants the other also.

In our traditional Punjabi culture, if any reason arose for the mother to consider leaving the home, she would never leave her child, even if she were cut into pieces. Her attachment to the child, her sacrifice for the child, kept the family intact.

Why are divorces taking place these days? Because people have not understood that marriage is a commitment with God. Whether a marriage takes place in a church, a mosque, a gurdwara, in a synagogue, in the open, or around a fire, a commitment is being made with Someone. The couple should understand that they are making a commitment with that Power which is doing everything for them. To divorce is to break that commitment, to break God's commandment, and this will not be good for people. Even if people do not believe in God, they should recall the commitment they have made to each other. In our traditional culture, our homes have been kept safe by the parents' love for the children and the understanding that their union is made by God. Parents also understand that their children will suffer badly if they separate, so they sacrifice for the sake of the children.

Nowadays people only put faith in their minds. If the mind so desires, one person goes one way and another person the other way. Anger arises unchecked and people become emotional and separate. If there is no control over the mind, what can be done? When a bridge is broken, what can shovels do? Now a crane will have to be brought in to rebuild these broken bridges.

God tells us not to injure another's feelings. Parents must first make a firm principle not to hurt each other. If you quarrel, both of you are miserable – the mother is crying by herself on one side and the father is crying by himself on the other. If you do not agree, it does not matter. Do not separate from each other in haste.

Instead, meditate upon God, control your anger, and recognize that it will be a great loss for the children if you do not remain together. If you grow in love and compassion, the foolishness within you will not be allowed to pass through your gates and hurt others. With this approach, both you and your children will experience peace. Even if clashing actions or angry thoughts have come between you, overcome them -let them pass. Thank God and ask God to bless that bad situation. Take His Love, His willingness to serve. Then remain together and give time to your children. Perhaps the day will come when your thoughts will change, and then you will see that there was no need for divorce.

This is very essential, for these are difficult times. With the blessing of God, this bad period will end, and a good period will come. This change can be brought through worship, through prayer, through meditation, through the remembrance of God. It is imperative to save the children. To do so, improve yourself: control your anger, your character, and your mind. Pray to God, and give love and time to your children. Receiving the intoxication of your love, they will abandon all other intoxicants.

A Child's Heart is Very Tender

To children and teachers from Banda Bahadur Public School, Mehrauli

Parents have placed these young children and their lives into the hands of their teachers and professors. It is a huge responsibility. Now we must consider how to develop these children. It is essential that some training about dharam should be imparted in our schools. For example, we must tell our children, that stealing is bad. Why? Because God is not happy when someone steals. Similarly, in your own way, you should make children understand that criticism is bad, that hurting others' feelings is bad.

Children's hearts are very soft. They can be moulded in whatever way you train them. Then by the time they go on to their universities, to their jobs, the training they received at this age will be fully recorded in their minds.

The greatest responsibility for training lies first with the parents. The behaviour of the mother and father influences their children. Even a child of six months has developed inner awareness. If the mother is angry, the gestures of the child's hands show that he knows his mother is angry.

Then when the child goes to school, there are two ways in which he gets such messages. One way is that he watches the actions of his teacher. Secondly he observes whether the teacher is actually practicing in his own life what he is teaches the pupils.

Do not consider children too small to understand. Their minds are quite developed. Today a child of eighteen years may have as much knowledge as a person of fifty years used to have. Why? They ask many questions. Even if you do not speak, they are watching you.

Therefore I say to you that it is with what we call religion, or dharam, that we develop our character, our life. With dharam, we develop justice; with dharam, we will be faithful and loyal. With dharam, we will rise. Dharam is not something separate from us; it is blended within us. Everything is hidden within us. As Guru Nanak said, "God kindled His light in you and thus you took birth."

Child, The Teacher of Humanity

To the Joint UNICEF-WCRP Conference on "World's Religion for the World's Children" at Princeton, New Jersey, U.S.A.

In this dark age of strife and struggles, whims and wars of states and statesmen, only the innocence, truth and simplicity of the child can save the world from the present crisis of civilization. The beauty of the child's smile is the source of our inner strength. This presence of the eternal innocence ensures the human continuum, charged with the task of peace and prosperity, happiness and bliss. We must learn from the child to forgive and forget, to play and persevere under all circumstances, for herein lies the hope of a better future, a future of brotherhood of all mankind, where love prevails, where peace reigns. We must learn from the child to live in harmony. We must learn from the child to respect the other, to interact with care and compassion.

The rights of all people are first the rights of the child. We must learn to listen to the child. We must learn the language of the child, which is able to discern the false from the true. The child communicates through gestures of affection, through the medium of sharing, a sharing of everything one has with the other. The other is transformed into his own by recognizing a community of playmates, companions, and friends. We must listen to the unspoken word of the child, for it is charged with the message of love and longings for a peaceful future, for the Child is the True Teacher of humanity.

A child represents three innate qualities: innocence, patience, meditation.

Mother and child: a relation of innocence, love and affection. The child smiles and the world of his parents is filled with happiness and bliss, a happiness and bliss that is most innocent. It has no logic; it is just there. The child is a source of happiness that does not require any reason, any selfish motive, any affair to be settled. It is love in the absolute sense of the term. It is innocence personified. The child smiles for no specific reason, with no specific need. She just smiles and the world smiles with her. It is the purest form of bliss, an ecstasy all saints and sages long to achieve.

The child as such is the greatest yogi, the most uninvolved, the most indifferent. The child is the real guru who teaches without any formal instruction, whose innocent gestures lead to the most penetrating truths of life and death.

Spend some time watching a child playing with her toys, with the plants in the garden, with her pups. There is a perfect correspondence between human instincts and the vibrations of nature. This is the highest form of harmony where all differences between the elements of nature and culture are eliminated. It is not simply a matter of hygiene or of pollution-free environment; it is primarily an affair of extreme intimacy, an almost sensuous relationship between the animate and inanimate world.

If we watch a child playing in the garden, the flowers, the plants, the toys made of clay or wood become vibrant beings for her. She handles them with care and love. She hugs them with affection and when she is angry, when her toys do not follow her instructions, she beats them. And when one of them breaks under the pressure, she cries at this unbearable loss. The inanimate and the animate lose their identity in this most human relationship.

Grown-ups have a lot to learn from this play. This innocent correspondence between nature and culture, between the world of God and the world of the child, presents an atmosphere of serenity and patience. For long hours, a child remains oblivious to the world of humans around. She creates her own world of sleep and dreams. There is no irritation, no impatient nervousness of the adult. Her needs are simple. She can wait for hours before her mother gives her milk. And just a simple, affectionate hug satisfies her and brings happiness to her mother. She not only does not disturb the atmosphere around her; her innocent gestures slow down the rhythm of all those adults who are in hurry, who presume to run this world.

A child's patience imparts harmony to this world of desires and divisions. In the presence of a child we forget the ever-increasing pressures of worldly involvements. By simple movements, by innocent gestures, by just being around, a child establishes divine harmony, an atmosphere of musical vibrations.

Not only is the child patient with the world, one has to be patient with the child. To enter the world of the child, we must stop and reflect. What a wonderful being is a child, the unity of environment; the harmony of souls she achieves. We begin to meditate upon this wondrous gift of God, this purest form of creation, the creation of life and growth and happiness; despite the inevitable problems, miseries and decay of life.

A child represents both the beginning and the end. Within concentric circles of being and nothing, of existence and extinction, one begins to slowly comprehend the turning of the wheel of mind and matter.

Within movements of happiness and hazards, we meditate upon the destiny of human beings that is so simple, like a simple gesture of a child, so innocent, like her innocent smile, and yet so complex, like the eternal mystery of her being.

A child is indeed the teacher of the adult. From her intuitive correspondence between nature and culture, we arrive at the highest levels of innocence, patience and meditation.

IV

Social Uplift

Poverty is not a permanent state. There is no such class or nation we can call 'the poor'.

Work hard, thank God and He will lift you out of poverty. This is my own personal experience.

The policies of the world are wrong. There should be no poverty.

Dharam is Social Work

To scholars and social welfare workers from India and Pakistan

True social work is that in which there is no self-interest, in which you work always for the benefit of others. Actually, all the prophets were social workers. The Prophet Muhammad had no selfish motives. People threw stones at him, but in his pure love he never backed away from distributing the blessings of Allah. When Guru Nanak came, people also threw stones and spoke rudely to him. But he kept on doing his social work, without any demands. Look at Jesus: He did not abandon his inner inclination for social work even when they crucified him. From the cross, he said, "Oh Father, forgive them; give Your love to them all." Look at Mahavir, Buddha, Moses, Guru Gobind Singh – all the prophets and messengers were social workers.

Now we have left the true dharam. Self-proclaimed religious authorities are residing in their own forts, bringing rebellion. Those who claim to speak for religion do not tell the people what the prophets have said but give their own versions. They have their own selfish motives: "How will I benefit? How will I be praised?" Therefore, we are now embroiled in disputes, for we do not understand what the prophets have said. We have no peace in our minds, and no true dedication to social work. We speak of it, but it is not within us. Social work will arise from within us when the light within us emerges. Peace will come throughout the world if we tell what the prophets themselves have said.

Rightly understood, dharam is social work. No religion teaches us to fight, no religion teaches divisiveness, no religion teaches hatred. They all teach us love.

SHARING WEALTH

Dharam tells us, "Share whatever you have." Gobind Sadan's wealth is for the people. Pilgrims continually come and whatever is here – our food, our spiritual wisdom – is shared with all. Those who work hard but still cannot meet their needs are given food, clothing, medical care, school fees, employment, weddings. Books and newsletters are printed to spread dharam. Thus the people's bodily thirst and also their spiritual thirst are satisfied. We hold big celebrations of the birthdays of all prophets – such as Jesus, Muhammad, Lord Krishna, Buddha, Sikh Gurus – for those days are very auspicious. All those times, God sent us a messenger in human form like us. He put His Light, His Voice into those forms, so that we could remember the Light that we have forgotten.

What is the difference between the income of a saint and the income of an ordinary person? The ordinary person uses all of his earnings for his small family. But the saint considers whoever comes to see him his family. He gives everything he has to everyone who comes. The greatest thing he has is enlightenment, and he shares that freely. If he has any worldly goods, he shares them also.

The system of Kirat is that you work hard and share whatever you have. If you have nothing, even then you share.

Remember that whatever food you eat comes from God. The clothes you are wearing also come from God. The electricity which is running the fans is also from God. If you boast, "See what a big house I have built!" then where is God? We should acknowledge and repay a little of our debt by sitting an hour or two each day in worship, in pleasing God.

Your wealth is purified by giving, your mind is purified by reciting Nam. It is a good thing to celebrate your birthday, for instance, by giving good food to others, distributing the surplus that is lying with you. If you give food in this life, you will be well fed hereafter. If you do not give anything here, your kitchen will be empty in the next life. We have a proverb: "The crops have been grown in advance in great quantities, so the person now eats to his full satisfaction." The good deeds which you have done – your service to others, your love – will always accompany you, and you will forever reap their benefits.

Always bear in mind that neither this body nor this mind belongs to us. These thoughts have been given to us by Someone else. He gives us thoughts, and thus we speak. He gives us this body also. It will remain for the period that He wants to retain it, and then it will be discarded.

People seek to protect themselves by every possible means and want to remain ever happy. But they have forgotten one point: There is a power within us that can provide us both happiness and protection. It is the power of God. There is no greater happiness, no greater safety than the enlightenment gained by meditating, by loving God.

Contentment is an inner matter. Dharam teaches us to regard everything as God's gift. A person who loves God says, "If there is hunger or sorrow, this is Your gift. If there is poverty, I am happy. If I am barefooted, I am still happy. If I have nothing, still I am happy."

A person sits in darkness, surrounded by his family, hoping that he will not die. He got a job, got married, produced children; then his life continually revolves around them, around and around like an oilseed press. Before long the angel of death comes and says, "Let us go." The person replies, "I am already tired." Actually, a person becomes exhausted before his death. His options, his tastes, his enjoyments, his attention are all finished, as if he were dead.

The Guru says, "An illusion has been created in the world, but to the minds of the people, it appears sweet." However, the attraction of wealth must reach a limit. A person may have been very fond of eating. He may eat and eat, but he has only one stomach. If there were several stomachs, one could be filled, then the next, and the next. But as it is, the person finds no enjoyment in anything.

Instead of worrying, "What will happen to my children? What will happen to my house? What will happen to my spouse?" come out of all that and think, "I must thank God for giving me children, spouse, house, energy and life." Meditate by elevating your mind, by having communion with God. Attraction towards God never fades. It may keep increasing for thousands of years. When you think of Him, there will be great attraction, but no other attraction will remain.

GOD'S SYSTEM FOR SOCIAL CHANGE

To the Russian Academy for Public Service Conference on the transformation of social systems

There is One Whom we call the Creator. Then there is all Nature, which He created – the earth, the waters, the trees, the animals. The Creator created all things and placed them in their natural state.

Who comes and upsets nature? Human beings. Nature is upset when humans' thoughts are not under their control, and when they are influenced by self-interest.

Therefore the first thing that must happen is that we must develop love in our minds – love for society, for God, for all of Nature. In order to develop that love within us, we must begin to love the Creator. When we begin to love that One who has created Nature, who is the Mover of all Nature, then He will give us His powers, His love and His wisdom.

If anger exists, it comes from within people. If there is crime in the world, it comes from within people. All in all, what spoils everything? Human thoughts. If people would begin to do what God has said, then everything will be affected. The main issue is this - Do we who seek to improve society believe what we are saying? Have we controlled our own thoughts? Once we have done that, then when we speak to people on this subject, vibrations will be created. That wave will travel through the air, through the trees, into the waters, and it will also enter our thoughts.

Therefore, in order to improve anything, people first have to improve their own thoughts, because it is people who have interfered with what has been created in Nature. God never interferes. Whenever Nature is spoiled, it is people who have spoiled it. But if there is intervention by a person who is full of love, service, and compassion, those qualities will continue to develop within the world and their effect will last forever.

Why do we have to maintain defense systems? Because people do wrong and countries do wrong; because people and countries create things which conflict with the natural order. Then the environment is spoiled, and people's minds are spoiled as well.

If our minds are filled with compassion and the willingness to serve – to serve not only people but also animals and plants – that system will never break down. It may last for thousands of years, hundreds of thousands of years, countless millions of years.

The greatest thing is that we must accept that there is Something behind everything which has been created. Behind them is the One who gave them birth. Where is He? He is within us.

Clean your mind

Before we speak on a subject, we must first develop that quality within ourselves, within our thoughts. Before we take any action, we should think, "Will we hurt anyone's feelings by doing that? Will we be depriving anyone of their rights? Will we be violating anyone's boundaries?" It was to introduce such thoughts, to speak about them and awaken them within people that the prophets, messiahs, and saints came.

If we want to eliminate the smoke from factories or the poisonous chemicals that are polluting the environment, we must first recognize that there is poison within us. We must first eliminate the poison within ourselves. What is this poison? Angry thoughts. Thoughts of denying others their rights. Thoughts of hurting others' feelings. How do our thoughts pollute the environment? Everything that issues from us enters the air and travels in the air, polluting the atmosphere. The waves of poison enter our surroundings and pollute them also. If anything goes wrong in a factory, polluting the water and air and harming health, that impact has also been created by human beings.

The solution for all these problems is to clean your own mind. Then nothing is difficult. You can stop theft. You can stop crime. You can create good systems, and people can live well. But first humans have to make their thoughts good.

Before you preach about anything, first correct your own thoughts. If you speak before an audience, desiring that there should be peace, that crime will cease, and that everyone will be blessed, it is very important to first develop those qualities within yourself. If we develop love, faith, and willingness to serve, when we speak society will be healed. Then wherever you hold a meeting, those qualities will heal the very earth at that place. The environment there will be healed, and your mind will be healed. Then you will truly feel that you did not waste your time. You will feel that you spent your valuable time in a good way and that you received something.

Love and peace do not come from books. They come from inside, from your heart. Speaking after reading books is quite different from speaking from your heart. Create love and peace inside. First control yourself. The door of God's love will never be closed to you.

Love is the basis

Good ideas come from God. These ideas will be developed only when you first develop them within yourself, when you first bring peace within yourself. Discard the anger that is inside you. Discard the fear. Discard the hatred. Discard your feelings that some humans are high and some are low. See God's Love within everybody, and see that Love within yourself also. And don't see it only in people – see God's Love in trees, in flowers, in the land. Why should you look towards God's Love? When that will appear within all of us, it will never end, and it never has.

If you have love inside you, you will create sound systems of law and order. If you have love inside you, those who are in charge of law and order will act justly. If love develops within you, your defense system, your finance system, and your management systems will all go well.

If we simply utter empty words about qualities which we do not possess, those words which flow from our tongue will not be good. They will not be full of love. If you speak of anything which is not full of love, faith, and willingness to serve, your effort will be wasted.

God is very loving. He does not place any demands on us. He has only one demand: that we love each other, love the trees, the waters, the air, the land. He says just one thing to us: "I have created only love. Do not create hatred."

In all the subjects you are considering in this conference, make this your central theme: Bring peace within yourself. If love and compassion develop within us, if violence is eliminated within us, then who will go out and kill the head of state? How can human beings kill other humans? How can humans needlessly kill animals or cut down trees? Only because we do not have peace inside us.

If the anger has not been eliminated within us, how can we speak of peace?

First discard the enmity from your mind. Discard distinctions between high and low. See God's Light in everything. Then as you speak with love, you will be healed within, and those who hear you will also be healed. The air will be healed as well, and wherever it travels, the trees and oceans will also be healed. Those waves of love will ascend to the stratosphere, and it, too, will be healed.

Become good yourself

Whenever there are good people, they are never in the majority. Instead, their strength lies in quality. Just as there is only one God, not two Gods, quality is very rare. Bad things are always in the majority.

May God bless you so that before you speak, you will bring forth within yourself those desired qualities about which you wish to speak. Then your words will affect the audience, and your meeting will be successful. Look within. Do you see any anger? If you do, and even if you speak against anger, your talk will have no effect. First remove your own anger. First judge the weaknesses within yourself. Don't judge anyone else.

God is ready to give us love, faith, and the willingness to serve. We have to be ready to receive them.

Be especially mindful of one thing: If you do anything good for someone, do not expect him to thank you. Service with expectation of thanks is a form of self-interest. If you did something good, that is fine, but keep moving ahead. Service and love will not be accepted if you want something in return for them. Love cannot be bought.

Keep doing good work, serving, and loving, and don't expect any thanks or praise in return. Just do it and forget it. Even if someone derides you, serve him also. If someone does not understand you, try to help him understand.

Systems are destroyed only by human beings, and only they can rebuild them. God always makes good systems. It is for us to follow them. Perhaps the ideas for this conference came into your mind because God put them there. God must be thinking that he wants to develop these ideas, for when He gives you good thoughts, He wants to develop them.

However, do not try to distribute that which you do not have. Make sure you understand this. If you have not developed love within yourself, don't try to distribute it to somebody else. If you do not have the desire to serve, don't talk about service. Only do those things that come from your own feelings. Then there will be no difficulty at all. People's minds will become good, crime will disappear, and people will understand that they are not to invade each others' territories. Why will these changes occur? Because you have prayed to God and have first become good yourself. People are ready to improve.

It is only people who destroy systems, and people are the only ones who can correct the damage. Look at those places where very few people have gone, where nature is undisturbed. In such places, people get peace and serenity. Wherever humans go, the first thing they do is destroy the place. But if you take good thoughts into a natural environment, it will not be destroyed.

Those people whose way is spiritual, visionary, loving and serving, did not hold big meetings to set up their programme. They received visions through meditation, through their love of

God. Whatever inspired thoughts then came into their mind, they not only spoke, but also practiced in their own lives.

If people discard self-interest, corruption will end. If people discard anger, defensive postures will end. Countries have set up territorial boundaries. We should try to send good things across these boundaries. This does not mean that we should break the boundaries and enter the countries to occupy them. If we did, war would inevitably ensue. If you deprive anyone of their rights, there will surely be fighting. Understand that we all want peace.

The people whom we want to attack also want peace.

Love creates love, and hatred creates hatred. From anger, enmity is created. Friendship is created from love.

Protection or Destruction?

To reporters from the Canadian Broadcasting Corporation

All the messengers have taken birth from love. Whomever you worship – be it Jesus, Moses, Abraham, Noah, Lord Krishna, Lord Ram, Guru Nanak, Buddha or any other messenger – their teachings were all based upon one point: that God creates love, creates compassion, and creates a great willingness to serve others. When Mahavir said, "Avoid violence," the meaning was the same: "Love."

When we fight with each other, we are acting contrary to God's message. When we oppose God's message, happiness, love, and feelings of service depart from us.

A person may simply devote his life to increasing his own pleasure. Or he may devote his thought and energy either to making people strong, or to destroying people. On the one hand, individuals are trying to save people by building hospitals, doing research into life-saving methods, producing medicines. On the other hand, individuals are putting energy and money into weapons research, into producing more deadly weapons. When these are used, people will be destroyed and medicine will not help. The great difficulty in the world today is that we are unable to decide whether we should spend for saving people or for destroying people.

Scientists have a great role in both efforts, for they carry out research in both saving and destroying lives. Today there is an ocean of progress on both fronts. The world's entire bank is being spent upon them. As broadcasters, you should pose the question: Will we benefit more from developing armaments or from saving lives?

We should make just one decision, i.e. to protect people, increasing their knowledge, their inner wisdom, their inner love. We should not use our brains for things which will harm people, will harm the trees, will pollute the air, will harm the animals. If we make this decision, all countries will become wealthy. There will be no dearth anywhere.

Everyone is nervous and frightened today. When they think of how many weapons have been produced, they worry that these might be used. After that, they worry, "Where will the cities go? Where will we go?" Death is hanging heavy on people's heads, and they are afraid.

It is the brains of individuals that bring peace, factories, comforts, and pleasure – but humans can also destroy everything. Wherever there is disturbance and conflict, it is brought by human brings.

Today the love in every heart has greatly diminished. This inner love is the most powerful thing which will keep us united, will teach us love for each other, will teach us good manners and sweet speech. This inner love is decreasing because each person has moved outside his realm of thought and exceeded his principles. He has mounted a horse upon which he does not apply his mind, and it has carried him away as he unwittingly urges it to speeds even he is unaware of. He does not know the outcome on his lineage, his city, his country. Ninety percent of the people have lost their love, and they do not even know it.

When a person crosses this limit, it is very painful for him to return. He has formed a habit, a bad habit. To get rid of that habit, he needs God's mercy and blessings. When he returns to his proper place, he recognizes, "All happiness was here. I was just uselessly sitting somewhere else."

Two things have shifted which are affecting people. In our religious institutions, many practices have entered which are not permitted by true religion. Similarly, many things have entered our justice system that law and order actually do not permit. There is a direct link between these two. It is the role of dharam to maintain law and order. When a person embodies dharam he will show compassion. He will not be corrupt, will not deprive others of their rights, will not hurt others' feelings. But if dharm departs, these virtues will also depart.

It is good to copy a good person. But these days people are imitating those who have failed. They say, "Look what a big house he has built." But he does not believe in dharam. He is a corrupt thief. Why then are you praising him? Praise those who have progressed by doing good. To speak out affects children and society as a whole. Say, "He is very honest and thus his fortune is good. If a person is bad he will become a prisoner and great blame will be placed upon him." Then those who hear will feel, "I do not want to become a prisoner."

Always be aware that goodness will never be in the majority. Its power will forever lie in quality. It is so powerful that it will shake the entire majority. This power lies in the mind. If a person's thoughts are strong, what does he care for evil? It may be there, but he will keep moving ahead in truth.

They say that the environment is being polluted by toxic chemicals in the air. But when a person speaks or thinks, he creates waves in the air. If it is an angry or criminal thought, it will produce waves of poison. If it is a loving thought, it will produce waves of love. At present people's thoughts are very poisonous. They are not under their control. Industrial pollution is much less harmful than the pollution created by peoples' thoughts.

Wherever there is conflict between countries, in societies, in offices, in households, it is a conflict of thoughts. The principle of religion is that whenever you meet anyone, you should meet them with such love that the person will continue to remember: "What a good person I met. We spoke so sweetly, and he has brought me so much love." If instead there was anger in an encounter, think of this: Misery is of our own making. God does not say, "Become miserable!" We make ourselves miserable.

If your body is in good shape and your thoughts are good, your whole being is well off. If your thoughts are good, you can progress whenever you like. Make your thoughts high and they will fly well. If your thinking is damaged from within, nothing will succeed.

Dharmic examples

Why has religion come into the world? To make people decent human beings. By dharmic training, people become proper masters of other forms of life and also set an example to other human beings. There is no other necessity for dharam. There were animals before, trees before, waters before. Religion came only to make exemplary human beings. From within human beings, Truth spoke. From within human beings came healing and training in righteousness, and humans became peaceful. It was also from within human beings that virtues and thoughts were spoiled, and individuals became bad examples. When a person's thoughts become bad, nobody can control them. Then his actions may become very dangerous, very destructive.

This is the present situation throughout the world. Destructive efforts have become so predominant that we must now make a conscious decision where to put our resources. Poverty can be completely eliminated, but we are instead wasting billions on those things which destroy human beings. Those things should be developed which enable human progress: housing, sustenance, meditation, hospitals. Then I think no one will be miserable anywhere.

But people do not think of this. They are fearful night and day: "If I become weak, my neighbour may occupy my house." By contrast, you can keep peace in such a way that your neighbour will not threaten your house. Jesus says, "Love your neighbour." Ask your neighbour, "Do you have anything to eat or is your food all gone?" Before having cloth sewn for yourself, ask your neighbour, "Do you need it?" Dharam teaches us this.

Jesus teaches us, "Look at the lily. Who has designed it? Look how soft it is, how beautifully it is designed, how beautiful is its colour. If my Father is caring for these flowers, creating their dress, creating their very life, then why do you worry? He will definitely take care of you as well. He will take care of your sustenance, your dress, your home." Even though you do not live in faith, still He provides for you.

Look at the flowers: They are happy even when it is raining. If a storm comes, even then they do not worry. The storm may beat them down, some to one side, some to another. But after it passes they will rise again and rejoin each other. We humans have not yet learned to do so.

For Peace, Open Your Inner Eyes

A message to interfaith organizers

It is on all your minds – in fact, it has become fashionable – to ask, "How can we unite our religions, so that there will be peace in the world?" This is a great mistake. Religions are already one. We ask, "How can peace come in the world?" But peace is not an outer thing; it is an inner thing.

Peace means that our evil desires, whatever they are, have all come under control, and whatever is good within us – such as enlightened wisdom – has been manifested. Peace means that compassion and love have emerged within us.

Violence is committed by individuals. It is individuals who speak of religions as being separate from each other. When there is peace within, there will be no separate religions nor will anyone revolt or commit crimes. We must first correct our own minds – but instead we say that there should be peace in the world.

The desire for peace is not new. The prophets have long said that there should be peace. But the Light of peace had already come forth within them. There was peace on their tongues, peace in their eyes, and peace in their thoughts. When they spoke, wherever they looked, or even when a thought crossed their minds, that power of peace also entered others.

But what is the situation today? We are speaking of things that we ourselves do not possess. Those of us who speak of peace must carefully consider, "Do we have peace?" Why should we advertise things we do not have? Why should we announce, "Come and purchase this!" Only that which we ourselves possess can be given to others – it can be shared and distributed. When we do not have peace, why should we speak of it?

Peace cannot be obtained by marching or by reading books or by delivering lectures. Peace is something within you.

All of you should turn your attention within. When we have all delved within ourselves, we will have no time for being angry with others, for hurting another's feelings, or for creating conflicts. Why? From morning to evening, we must fight with our mind in order to control our thoughts. We will be too busy to lecture or fight with others.

At present we are all idle. After reading our scripture we say, "My prophet is greater than yours." Why? This is against the teachings of our religions. It is against the commandments of the prophets. It is also against humanity.

Understand this well: There has never been any prophet or messiah who has said that God is two, peace is two, or that there are two different loves or two compassions. They all say one thing. From Adam to today, God is giving the same message through all the prophets.

However, the religious authorities will never tolerate the coming of truth. Up to now, religious authorities have never explained religion as it was taught by the prophets and messiahs. The religious authority always says, "There is no other prophet like my prophet." When we say this, it creates anger and injures the feelings of others – and that is a great act of violence. Now the same people who are trying to unite religions are the ones who have created the divisions in the first place. Only that person can be considered a religious authority who reads the scriptures of the prophet, personally practices the message contained therein, and conveys the same to others. The same orders apply to religious authorities as they do to the public. The prophets have all said, "Do not become leaders – become servants."

If we do not convey the correct message of the Holy Qu'ran, the Bible, the Gita, the Guru Granth Sahib, we ourselves are like darkness obscuring the sun. The truth is that God whom you are seeking outside is within you. Our message is this: Look for Him within. He is talking. He is giving love. He is watching. He is also laughing. He is doing everything. But you must see Him with full inner vision. As Guru Gobind Singh said, "God is manifest and present everywhere." The prophets did not just say this. They first saw God and then spoke.

Lord Jesus said, "This is my Father." He was not just speaking in the air. He used to talk to God and receive commandments from Him.

Lord Muhammad did not merely say, "There is one God." He was always speaking with God.

When Lord Buddha said, "Truth," why did he call God Truth? If we can see clearly, all the prophets have referred to God as Truth. They have all said that God is Truth and Love. Lord Buddha said, "Speak truth and love, and do not commit violence."

There was not only one prophet who said, "My Allah is Master of the skies and Master of the earth, Master of the universe." This means that God exists in everything. If this is so, then why should there be violence? If God is Truth, then why should there be violence?

Prophet Muhammad called Him the Light of the earth, the skies, and the universe. He said this Light is continually being showered inside.

Guru Nanak said, "All are part of my community. No one is an outsider."

When every prophet has taught us these same lessons, why don't we act accordingly? Our inner feeling, our inner love for God, our inner vision also tell us, "God is one, love is one, service is one, and human beings are also one."

Why does a religious authority take pleasure in repeatedly quarreling? Because you people listen to him attentively when he addresses you, but he himself is the biggest offender. When the teacher speaks incorrectly, how can the students become good? When the doctor is performing the wrong operation, how can the patient be saved?

These days the main issue is that the operations are wrong. Boundaries and fortresses are being preached, but it is not being taught that God is Light, that God can be seen everywhere, that God gives light everywhere.

Why should we try to confine Him? We should stress this point: This Light is within everybody. We need not close our eyes. They need to be opened so that we can delve deep inside.

Peace will not come by marching, nor by delivering lectures on scriptures that you have read but are not practicing. I am not alone in saying this. All the prophets have spoken alike.

I am not sending you this message to attract you, or to make you recognize me as guru or pir (Muslim saint). I am sending it to urge you to accept and believe whatever the messengers and messiahs have said. It is not my mission to make you join me by breaking your connection with them. I have never uttered a single word which has not been said before. I am only referring to those things which have already been said by the Prophet Muhammad, Lord Jesus, Moses, Abraham, Lord Buddha, Lord Mahavir – by all the prophets. I just repeat them again and again. Why? Because the human mind forgets very quickly. I am just reminding you of those things by writing to you, so that you will remember Him and not forget His teachings.

I am not interested in creating a separate religion, or in claiming myself to be separate, because God exists already. God's Love already exists. The message of God has already come through the prophets. I just want to affirm that message so that you will thoroughly understand it and become firmly committed to it.

One who believes in Jesus does not commit violence. One who believes in Hazrat Muhammad does not commit violence. He says, "We are all brothers, and if one brother kills another, how can Allah be happy?"

None of the prophets have said, "You should fight." None have said, "Be angry." None have said, "Disrespect others." None have said, "Deprive others of their rights." None have told us to speak words to others that incites violence.

You must therefore stress: Whenever you read any of your holy books, don't just set the book aside after reading it. After reading it, practice what you have read. Nothing has been written in scripture which would divide us. Only that which unites is written therein. What we humans have spoken is a different matter; people quarrel among themselves. But in the scriptures, it is written. "Look at the flowers, even there is the Creator. Look at the trees, at the mountains, the rivers, the seas – the Creator is there. If you want to see the Creator, see Him in all Creation."

I want to reaffirm that which was taught by Jesus, by Moses, by Muhammad, by the Vedas, that which Lord Krishna said in the Bhagavad-Gita, that which Lord Rama said in the Ramayana. I want to reaffirm those words and pray to God, "Oh Paramatma (God), remind them of Your messages which You have sent, because they keep forgetting them." This is my mission.

All of us should make it our mission to go deep inside and open our inner eyes. If we look clearly with our inner eyes, we will see that God is one, religion is one, and the message is one. Jesus only did what had already been written in the Torah. If he had wanted to create separate factions, why would they have written about Jesus in the Torah, telling that he would come, would go to Jerusalem, and would be crucified? Jesus did all those things to fulfill what had already been written by his forefathers. Perhaps he rode into Jerusalem on the back of a donkey because it had been foretold. He was fulfilling whatever his ancestors had already said.

Hazrat Muhammad was also fulfilling whatever had already been said. Even Moses was doing whatever the elders had written in the older scriptures. Lord Rama went into exile because it had already been written; he had to do what he did to fulfill the sayings of the sages.

No prophet would distort the messages of earlier prophets. Rather, they sacrificed themselves to fulfill those messages. They gave their time and energy, gave up their comforts, because they felt, "Whatever our ancestors have said should be followed exactly."

Therefore you should all sit and think, "What are we doing? Why are we wasting so much of our time to no advantage?" First heal your mind, and when healing comes on your tongue, others will be healed by your very speech. But instead, what we do is very bad. We advertise whatever is on our minds in a loud voice, like hawking wares which are not in our shops. We call, "Come, buy!" But our shop is empty. Whoever visits that shop goes away empty-handed. If nothing is there, just close the shop. Take peace from inside. Then you need not speak. Peace will be reflected in your movements; peace will emerge from your actions.

The prophets did not speak to please the people. They spoke innocently and people were healed. If you look carefully, every prophet has been a healer.

We should not be in doubt. When we say, "All religions should become one," we are speaking from ignorance, because religions are already one. We say, "Unity must be created," but unity has already been created. We are dividing it.

Gobind Sadan's programme is to repeat whatever has already been said by our elders, by the prophets, messengers, the Vedas. By God's grace, we should only repeat the messages of the prophets so that people will firmly believe them. They have said so much – How can we say anything more? They have not left anything out. There is nothing new to be said about God. What new message can we give? But we should accept what has been said. Faith is a great thing.

It is very essential at this time to follow the teachings, because the present upheaval has been brought on by religion. Actually, it has not been brought on by religious teachings, but by the religious authorities. Why quarrel? Look at the incident that just happened yesterday at Charar-i-Sharif (the revered shrine of the Sufi saint Sheikh Noor-ud-Din Noorani in Kashmir, burned by militants in 1995) Why destroy the place of a great saint? That saint used to say, "Allah is everywhere." By destroying his shrine, what are we trying to achieve? Do we want to destroy the name of Allah or of that saint? A saint is one whose ego has already been annihilated and within whom God's Light has come. The voice of God can never be annihilated. To attack the saints will only bring God's wrath. It is neither good for you nor for society.

So many such cases have occurred. You should all understand clearly that there is no difference between the person who does something wrong and the person who does not speak up; no difference between the person who says a bad thing and the person who accepts it. To commit a crime is wrong, and to see a crime being committed and accept it is also wrong.

You must think: Religious teachings are not different. But keep away from religious authorities, because at this time they are using their full force to maintain their wealth and make you forget God. We need to tell the religious authorities to only preach what is written in the scriptures. We want to say to them, "Don't say anything from your personal point of view. Let the people live in peace. The messengers who have come from God will never be separated. Why are you wasting your time? The family of prophets will never follow your views. Their programs have already been set. Their messages have already been given. That family will remain together. Moses and Jesus will remain together, try as you may to separate them. Why are you wasting your time? They are one. One messenger speaks of God; another speaks of Allah. It is only a difference of language, but they are saying the same thing.

The major point you must all understand is that religion is one, love is one, humanity is one, and existence is one. We should not be separated. We should all be wise.

We should not waste our time. At present, there are great needs in the world: People need homes, people need food, people need clothing. We should not be wasteful by going to big hotels and such places to hold seminars. We go there and speak. Fifteen to twenty lakhs (hundred thousand) rupees are spent, and we return to our homes. Our subject is, "How can religion be made one?" Why are you wasting this money? With the amount you spend there, twenty to twenty-five houses could be constructed, or two hundred to four hundred children could be educated. Look how much is spent on airfare? What are we all doing?

There is one benefit of seminars –we meet each other, shake hands, talk to each other, and eat rich foods. But if we say that peace will come from this, then forget it, all of you. There is nothing in this which can bring peace.

Those who brought peace were not sitting in big buildings or speaking from high thrones. If Jesus's gown was torn, he still wore it and preached. If he had no shoes on his feet, he walked barefoot and preached. But wherever he went, wherever he looked, the earth was blessed, the trees were blessed, the waters were blessed, and the people were blessed.

Look which way you are going. You are all well educated people. Come to your senses. Don't close your eyes. It's not good to keep your eyes shut. All of you must use your minds and show love to everyone.

On Enlightened Development

To Gobind Sadan's International Forum on "Enlightened Development: Making Capitalism Inclusive"

For enlightened development, we must first develop our own consciousness. Everything must start with meditation. Without meditation, you will not be able to recognize what is happening in the world, you will not perceive spiritual power, and you will not even understand your own nature. Meditation is such a power that you can understand what goes on around you, perceive the force within you, and even understand every person's nature.

I will share this small example that you can see for yourselves. When I was a young man and did not even have a beard yet, the vision came to me that Russia would one day become a very spiritual country. I had never even heard of Russia. When I asked someone about Russia, they told me, "If you take the name of God in Russia they will kill you." But I told them what I had seen in my vision. And when I went to Russia I found proof that spiritual power is literally erupting in Russia. There was so much evidence that even in the average person I could see spirituality. I could see love, and faith, and truth within each one.

The whole world is crying, "Let's get rid of poverty," and every country, every organization puts forth its own speakers, but poverty still continues unabated. So let us understand that poverty does not really exist. With full faith, I want you to realize this.

I am not from a rich family. I came from a very poor family where we never had enough to eat. But I made up my mind that I should not beg from anyone. I thought, "Let's get up and work, share with the people, and feed ourselves." Now I can tell you that I have a surplus of everything, and everything I have is for the people. We organize medical camps, bring doctors, provide food, and I go and preach for the uplift of those in need.

Raise yourself so high that God comes and asks, "What can I do for you? What do you need?" Why run after people? I have full faith that one day the current conditions will change and you yourselves will see a change in the world. This is God's mission and mine.

One day it will happen because God wants poverty to be eliminated. God will listen to your prayers.

When I went to Russia I saw that people don't work. They think, "The ruler will give us a home, feed us, and take care of all our needs." That is why poverty has spread throughout the country. Forget these ideas. The rulers are our management. Cooperate with them, work along with them, and they too will change and wealth will come if you begin to work. What is government? We are all government.

There is no poverty. This is something we have created. It has no basis, no roots. Get rid of it. Share with those in need. Those who become rich are sitting comfortably on their wealth. Why? That is not God's teaching.. What are you going to do hoarding your wealth? If one of your children is irresponsible, he will misuse all your wealth and you will be left with nothing. And when you die, you will be beaten. They will tell you, "You never did anything for the world." Here people may salute you, but there you will be beaten. They will question you, "When you received all this, you were told to share. Why didn't you do it?" Share your thoughts. Share your work. You will have to work. If you don't work, even those things which you have will one day be exhausted. Share whatever God has given you. Work with the poor and share among yourselves.

If you want to become good human beings, you will live by this simple formula: Respect those who have more, make friends with those on the same level, and show kindness to those beneath you. You will never be disappointed. You will always live happily.

People are responsible for the events in the world. One good person stands up and the whole world changes. The majority has never brought change to the world. Whenever the world has changed, it is because of those of quality. What is the majority? Sheep are standing in the field. One lion appears and roars and half of them die from fear. So do not look at numbers; develop quality. Take God's blessings. Your door to God is closed, and you have left the door of your mind wide open. Your mind will only create worry for you. You cannot see beyond your own limited thoughts.

Share all you have. Don't grasp it tightly to yourself. You do not know what will happen tomorrow. The Gurus say, "After a person dies, we don't even keep the dead body for a few minutes." "Even the little hut is blessed where one sings God's praises. The mansions are worthless where God is forgotten." Those who try to clutch their wealth become so bound they cannot even breathe. Be free. See God everywhere. Guru Gobind Singh said God is omnipresent – "In the water, in the earth, near and far." Jesus said, "My Father is the Ruler of all creation. He is providing everything that we need. You are all so worried about your dress. Look at the lily – who gave it clothes? You want to look beautiful. See how soft and beautiful, how delicate the lily is."

Have faith. If you don't have faith, you have nothing. If you have faith, God will walk with you.

The Power of Women

Why are women left behind? Why should women consider themselves weak? All women need to do is stand up for their rights. In the writings of the Sikh Gurus, God is sometimes referred to as the female Power, sometimes as one's closest girlfriend, and sometimes as Mother of the World. Here in India, God is often referred to as Mother, with 108 female forms, all of whom are avtars (incarnations of God). The blazing splendour of God's Power is manifested in female form, as Bhawani (form of the Goddess). Women have thus been historically highly respected in India.

A daughter is brought up to be a good manager by her mother, and then learns by the requirements of running a household, raising children, and taking care of guests. She naturally becomes a capable manager.

God has made a woman fertile like the earth. Everything is born from the earth. When great scientists, philosophers, doctors, prophets, saints come into the world, they all are given birth by women. God has decided, "I will make a woman the medium." The mother is also the child's first teacher. I always carry this thought in my heart, "If my mother had not come, where would I be? If my mother didn't exist, how would I be able to share this message? If Jesus had no mother, then how would Jesus have preached?"

That is why a woman is blessed. She does not need the blessing of a man. She needs the love of man; but blessings are already hers.

Some women ask, "Why have women seldom been accepted as prophets?" Actually, the woman has a higher status than a prophet, for it is she who gives birth to prophets. One who creates something is very powerful.

Never has a prophet taken birth through a man, only through women. Men may make as many positions for themselves as they like, but God has specially blessed women in this way. We know that Mary was directly blessed by the Holy Spirit in order to conceive Jesus.

There is a story of Rabia (a great eighth century Muslim saint of Iraq) told in the book *Tazkarat-ul-Aulia.* Many people, including great male prophets and saints, have been to Mecca to perform their obeisance at the sacred Ka'aba (Holiest sanctuary of Islam built by Abraham and Ismael in Mecca). But when Rabia went, the Ka'aba itself traveled ten miles from Mecca in order to receive her. At that same time, the saint Hazrat Ibrahim Azam went to Mecca for his pilgrimage, but the Ka'aba was not there. A voice from above said to him, "The Ka'aba has gone to receive a humble lady, Rabia."

Guru Gobind Singh chose Five Beloveds. There was no woman among them. But woman is higher than the Five Beloveds, for she has given birth to them. And it was Guru Gobind Singh's wife, Mata Jito ji, who sweetened the amrit (nectar) with which the Five Beloveds were baptized, to bless and temper their characters with love.

There were so many people whom Jesus rewarded, but he selected Mary Magdalen to anoint him with oil. When he was resurrected after his crucifixion, she and some other women were the first people to see him. God did not send a man with them, because God did not want to give that high rank to a man.

When Buddha was practicing meditation to the point of near-starvation, it was a woman who brought him khir (rice pudding) to eat. There were so many men around him, but it was a woman who fed him.

In Hindu scriptures, there was a time when the world was overrun by demons. At that time, God sent His Power through a woman, Durga Mata (the Goddess). She killed all the demons and restored goodness in the world.

If women want to become prophets themselves, there is no obstacle. But if a woman becomes a prophet, she may be downgrading the blessings of God. God has made woman even higher. Women are the creators of prophets.

"I am a simple farmer who loves God. Work hard and share with those in need and God will fulfill all your desires"

Plowing Gobind Sadan's fields, 1971 *(Ralph Singh)*

Fruits of God's bounty - Walking through Shiv Sadan's wheat (c. 1990)

In Shiv Sadan's record sugarcane fields

Supervising sugar cane planting with Gyani ji and Gurdev Singh

Babaji in fields
(Studio Pammy)

Giving books to the poor children at Shiv Sadan school

Dr Karan Singh and Harvinder Singh with Babaji dedicating Shiv Sadan

Speaking to sangat in Shiv Sadan

May You Be Blessed by God, Who is Giving Light to All Creation

A Message to women working for God's Mission

Always maintain your desire to serve, and speak the truth. Do not make any worldly demands in return for sharing God's blessings and God's Name. Do not make any demands in return for speaking about God. You should ask only one thing of God: Let everyone become good, become loving, let everyone desire to serve and understand God. This should always be your desire.

Women can do so much for their families, for society, and for their children. A woman may become a great teacher for her children. She can set a great example for her family.

There are no two ways about it: God has given women a very high place. Whenever prophets, messiahs, and messengers were sent by God, they came to earth through a woman. It was woman who gave them birth in the world; God chose a woman to give them form. If we look at it clearly, a woman is a gift from God. Whatever power God chooses to manifest in a person will definitely come through a woman. Whenever a great scientist, philosopher, prophet, or messiah was created, God has never set women aside and used any other method to bring them into the world.

Women express their devotion for God with great love. They are also devoted to their families and thus give them peace. In whatever social role they hold, God also gives them love and peace to bring to their workplace. But this only happens if they have already developed these qualities within themselves.

If we were to develop a team of workers for God, we would first prepare the ground. The better the soil and the more nutrients given, the better the plants will grow. Similarly, when you speak, the more your thoughts are filled with love, faith, and dedication to service, the more your message will spread like a great tree.

Don't waste a lot of time looking at the crime and sins and oppression in the world. Instead think, "How much are we doing to further God's work? What are we doing to alleviate people's fear?" Take God's support and then look for chances to share God's message with people; look at how much work you can do. Thus that tree will spread its branches so broadly that it will give shade to all.

In truth, ideas which are devoid of love, of service, and of kindness will not have much influence. The better the workers and the better their thoughts, the more goodness will spread.

Evil is always in the majority. In such people, there is no love and no sense of service. Those qualities exist only in a few people, but their influence will be great and their message will spread. Their influence will spread in society, in schools and colleges, in their countries. Bad influences will be cast aside, and darkness will be dispelled as the light comes forth.

Whenever you have the opportunity to speak to others, always turn your thoughts toward the holy ones of God. Take their love; take their blessings before speaking, for God is very gracious. After you receive God's goodness, speak. Talk to people in society, in schools, among your friends, within your family. Goodness will spread and peace will emerge in your country, in your society, and in your homes.

Always keep two things clean: your mind and your body. It is as necessary to keep your mind clean as it is your body.

Those people are always blessed who speak of love, who teach others to love, who help unite people, who tell people about the light and love of that great Power, and who themselves embody those teachings.

The more you speak with love and explain with love, the more people will be healed. Peace will enter them. When a person speaks with love, even though we cannot see it, the other person is being healed. Speak from your heart, with love, and forget the result, and very good things will come of it.

Tell everyone to direct their attention to God. Their disappointments and their difficulties will automatically be relieved by God.

Make your life an example of God's teachings, as brought by all the prophets. I expect all of you to practice those things that you will instruct others about from the love within yourself. As a result you will never be worried, and the people you meet will be healed.

Charge to the Press: "Incite Love and Truth, Not Hatred and Falsehood"

To a press conference in Lucknow, India

When I spoke on national television in the Soviet Union, I gave this message: "God is a Force of love, of kindness, who gives us energy and compassion. You cannot leave that Force and expect people to work for good. It will never happen."

When priests use the name of God for their personal benefit, they are working against God's will. Similarly, some religious authorities have opposed the prophets' teachings. Then they build temples to commemorate the prophets' memory and sit there to live off the offerings that the faithful bring. They turn religion into a business. They give education, medicine, clothing, and food to people in need – and then when the people have become attached to them, they tell the people to convert to their religion. Instead of following the teachings of their own prophets, they try to establish a majority. They use obscure spiritual terms that are not well understood to manipulate the people to their own advantage. This is not religion; this is not dharam. Dharam is love, without any selfish motive. In God's house there is no policy, no cleverness, no business, and yet this is the way religion is run today.

Question from the press: The clergy have become an extension of the political system. They are being bought by the politicians, so they are not giving the true message of religion. What is the solution to this problem?

Babaji: I sense that everybody does feel that we have been wrong. If this is put forth on the television and newspapers, tens of millions of people will receive the message. Truth is very powerful: when placed before people, no one can deny it.

It isn't that all people are bad. The populace in general is very good. There are only a few mischievous people who continually mislead the public. But it is not so difficult to change this situation. You all know that this system put forth as religion is something which humans have created. It has nothing to do with God. If a building has a firm structure, it is very difficult to shake it. But the structure by which priests take alms for themselves has no base at all.

You cannot blame this situation on the politicians. It is actually our fault. We act as if we have no sense and mindlessly accept religious "authority," following like sheep. Give it a little thought – A place of worship should be a place for enlightenment, for developing inner wisdom.

The real struggle going on in the world today is between the founders of each religion and their followers. The disciples have turned themselves into gurus, and there are no followers left. God's messengers say one thing and their disciples say the opposite. If you place the true spiritual heritage before the public, peace will ensue.

Religious "leaders" have all come under the influence of worldly power. Why? God only knows.

There is no political figure who has not visited Gobind Sadan. No one feels that this is a place for only one group or religious sect; everyone comes. What is our relationship with these political figures? I offer them spiritual teachings and give them Jaap Sahib. I tell them, Here, recite this scripture, take God's blessings, don't mislead people, and don't fool yourself. Whatever you give to someone else will definitely come back around to you. Therefore, send good things to others.

Why do people bow before these worldly powers? It is beyond me. After all, they are just human beings. They are first graders who are just picking up their books for the first time. They really don't know anything about dharam. If the principal of the school goes out to receive these new students with garlands, how will the students feel, and what does that say about the principal? It is possible that the religious figures' motive in garlanding politicians is to attract a lot of people and collect a lot of money. What else could it be?

The greatest danger comes from inciting people against each other. The whole world is aflame. Why should people take pride in adding more wood to the fire? But to talk to people about meditation, to teach that people of all religions should live as brothers and sisters, that the message of all the prophets is the same – this is the responsibility of us all, because this is the greatest need of the time. Let us bring home those things which are in short supply, not those things of which we already have a surplus.

There is always plenty of hysteria, anger, and fighting. Husbands, wives, children, neighbours – everyone is fighting. We need to be told how we can learn to live together. The prophets of all religions have so much to teach us on this subject. If someone speaks the truth, you should all support him. Let us stress those things from which eternal life will spring.

Work Hard and Meditate and the Path to Peace will Emerge

To participants in Gobind Sadan's Forum on Enlightened Development

There is a movement in the world today to convert people to another religion. From my youth, I have opposed this practice. I have opposed this. What religion is there to change? I have been against this practice from my childhood, when I did not even have a beard.

We have given great respect to all religious traditions. You will see that people pray to Jesus twenty four hours a day here. They stand and sing his praises. So when people say that we should become Christian, I ask, "What do you mean by Christian? Do you mean that I have to follow your orders? I don't wear a cross, and I'm not a Christian, but Jesus came and met me here. He gave me great blessings, great boons."

I'll give you a small example. Two young people came. They were both blind. I told Mary to take them to Jesus, and tell Jesus very simply and directly, with love: "You are the one who gives sight to the blind, and makes the cripples climb mountains. Please do the same for them. They need to see." Now they can, for this is the nature of Jesus.

The scientist and the one who loves God have very much in common. You will see that after a little while, scientists will discover fourteen planets where very good human beings live. Their science is very advanced.

So remain happy and laugh. Don't think about your age. You will see that soon the average person will live 100 years. There are many 90-year-old people today who are enjoying their full lifestyle. But just keep faith. If you doubt, you will become worried.

Question: When you speak about work, do you mean work with our minds, thinking, or with our hands?

Babaji: Link your minds to God and work with your hands. If you do not apply your minds, what kind of work will you produce? But if you do not work, your minds will create mischief for you.

Question: We look at the conditions of the world – terrorism and conflicts, poverty, environmental degradation, pollution of the landscape, air pollution, major climate changes. Even though we scientists have shown that we humans have made major mistakes, the people still continue with their current practices and do not accept this lesson. What future can we expect?

Babaji: Work and meditate and you will find the path out. The darkness will run away. I see good times ahead. The more the world is burning, the more rain God will send to put out the fire. I do not want you to worry. Everything will change.

One day the three great powers will come together. Write it in your diaries: China, Russia, and America. When the three come together, the times will begin to change for good. No one will be left out.

Question: Maharaj ji, I am so happy sitting among these brothers and sisters. You have brought these people together but it doesn't seem that they have come from Russia. They have been my brothers and sisters for many births. It feels that they really are our family and that the borders of the world have disappeared. Please bless us that our sense of differences goes away so we can live together as one family.

Babaji: What you are feeling will increase. That feeling will not leave.

Qustion: Our media are sick. They only show the dark side of life, the wars, the killings, and the crime. There are many good things happening as well. How do we cure the media so they project a better society?

Babaji: They will change. They are writing about our work here, for instance. First change yourself. When they see how you have changed, they will also change. Instead of worrying about how to change them, why not spend the time changing yourself? Then you will see the change in the world.

Question: When people receive a certain level of income, beyond their basic needs, they develop culturally and spiritually. Then in poorer countries, we have found that people have to spend all their time thinking about tomorrow, simply worried about survival – with the exception of India. Despite the fact that they are poor, many of the people here are happy and enlightened. How and why does this happen? And what can we learn from them?

Babaji: They are like tigers. A tiger may live alone in the jungle. Whenever he steps out of the jungle and roars, the other animals tremble with fear. Don't think of people as poor. They are like tigers, and those who aren't worried about material things make very loyal friends. You can learn from those who are happy even though they may be poor that you should also be happy and not worry about what you have.

V

Enlightened Governance

Truth is never in the majority. It is not a matter of quantity – its strength lies in quality.

By the grace of God, one person alone makes a scientific discovery, one person alone changes his society, one person alone changes a country.

Dharam and Public Policy

To political leaders

Guru Nanak has stressed that for good governance, "Oh king, proceed with truth and good moral character." He also said, "The ruler must be just. Make this your goal: Please the people and work for the people."

A person who remains aloof from the allure of money and love of his own praises shall rule the world. If anyone praises you, immediately say, "You should understand that whatever quality is in me belongs to God. Whatever energy or willpower is in me has been given by God. Nothing is mine." When you leave everything to God, your glory will shine like the sun. Whatever obstacle arises in your path, God will demolish it, for nothing is as powerful as God.

If God desires, He can turn a poor person into a ruler, or make a ruler a pauper. If His kind gaze falls upon a person, He can make him the ruler of the whole universe. If He diverts His merciful gaze, that same person will become poor.

Guru Gobind Singh, after sacrificing his father and his whole family, remained committed to one theme: "Oh God, this is all Your mercy, Your kindness, Tav prasad." At one point during his fight against Mughal oppression He was walking barefoot through thorns and cold, sleeping in the open on the hard ground, and his clothes were torn. His four sons had already bravely died for the cause, his besieged army had been decimated, and he had become separated from his remaining followers as they traveled by dark. But his enlightenment could not be destroyed. The light within him was shining the same as ever. Happily, he said, "Today I have no weapons, no horse, no army, no carpet. But Oh Khudavand (Master), Your Mercy is with me. I am victorious, because you are standing by me. To sleep under warm quilts is like a disease if You are not with me. To live without You is like living among cobras. Oh God, living on bare ground with You is better than living in fine palaces, for without You they are like burning ovens.

To the tyrants, he said a very great thing: "When my mind is unafraid; how can you frighten my body? I have become fearless and without enmity. My desire is that God may also give you enlightenment."

Guru Amar Das, from his enlightened wisdom, said "The world is burning. Please save it by Your mercy." The Guru appeals to God. "The whole world is suffering under fear, under pressure. I have only one request: Please free all people, so that their burden may be shed. Cast Your light upon the rulers so that they may love You and deal lovingly with the public."

Guru Nanak made no demands of God, and to our amazement, Guru Gobind Singh also made no demands. Where there was danger or great oppression, he ran headlong toward it. One thinks, "It is amazing. He has no fear of danger. He always faces danger and removes the threat." He has instructed you to do the same: "Oh my children, worry for others, not for yourself. Be concerned where the honour of the daughters and sisters of the country is threatened. Be concerned when anyone is deprived of their rights, and pray that God will give you strength to set them free."

So my children, if you move graciously among the public, if you combine public policy with dharam, and speak of dharam in government, the very earth will kiss your feet.

Appeal to Leaders: You are Misleading the Public

Today all of you leaders, whether you call yourselves social reformers or religious preachers, want to promote yourselves in the country. For your own sake, you speak in large gatherings and blame each other for corruption. You waste all your energy throwing mud on each others' parties, but we see no improvement. Why? Your own minds are rebelling against the orders of the great teachers and prophets. When you yourselves are not ready to listen to and follow the orders of our elders, how can you lead the nation?

You must first study the scriptures of the country and test yourselves. Peer into your inner selves. Sweep under your own seats. You blame each other, raising your voice about corruption. If we look closely, there are no leaders, no matter which side they may belong to, who can escape this blame. All are liable to be punished.

Today it is necessary to obey the orders of Guru Nanak Dev ji and the commandments of Guru Gobind Singh ji, who even sacrificed his small children in order to establish these principles of justice. Guru Nanak Dev Ji says, "By conquering your mind, you can conquer the whole world." Why is our mind to be conquered? Because our mind is the manifestation of the Light. We must recognize our Source.

Your souls are not committing corruption; your minds are doing it, because your minds have slipped. You put your energy into obtaining others' women and amassing others' wealth. You are not practicing what you preach. You are misleading the public. Our young people have gone astray from the path of righteousness, because their leaders have forgotten their duty.

Our teachers and prophets have shown us great wide open roads. "Earn your living by honest means and share with those in need," said Guru Nanak. They have taught us how to live in a high and pure way. But you are traveling on the wrong path. They have said, "Rise in the ambrosial early hour and chant God's Holy Name." Start your daily routine work only after meditating. Restrain your mind against doing evil. Control lust, anger, greed, ignorance, egoism, and bad thoughts. The Fifth Guru said, "There are five evils within me, and I am only one humble person: O Protector, please defend me from them."

Our minds have been polluted by the dirt of innumerable past lives. How can this filth be cleansed? Only by chanting the God's Holy Name (Nam). So accordingly, the only thing Guru Nanak Dev ji brought from the Immortal One was God's Holy Name. He said, "In the house of Nanak, there is only Nam. " Guru Nanak further said, "In this present age only Nam will save you. Kali Yuga has come; sow the seed of Nam."

Today we cannot be saved by speeches or by criticizing each other. Improve yourselves. What to speak of your states and your country, improve your own homes. This will be a great achievement. In your speeches, not only do you criticize each other; you do not even spare the prophets. The Guru is addressing you very people when he says, "You can not even offer us a small palm full of water, but you criticize that Being who brought forth the Ganges."

Then you speak of high and low and of castes. To which high caste did Valmiki (the sage who wrote down the Ramayana) belong? Bhagat Ravidas, Bhagat Kabir, Namdev, Sain – you know full well about the castes of these saints (all were from low classes). Guru Gobind Singh saw all humanity as one caste. He introduced us to the One who pervades each leaf, who is omnipresent and visible everywhere, who is nearer than our hands and feet, who cares for our very breath, our food, our drink, and our sleep. On what basis can you criticize the creation of the Creator? Guru Gobind Singh taught us to take care of others. He sacrificed everything to save our religion and others' faiths as well. Baba Deep Singh, Bhai Mani Singh, Bhai Mati Das, Bhai Dayala, and hundreds and thousands of great martyrs sacrificed to make our history a beacon of light to show us the path. They are the living examples of our history.

I was very disappointed when I went to Punjab. The youth have forgotten Sikhism. No one knows even the names of our ten Gurus, four Sahibzl©ade (martyred sons of Guru Gobind Singh), and Panj Piyaras (first members of the Khalsa), not to mention the remaining history.

This is the responsibility of the management committees. The offerings in the Gurdwaras are meant for preaching righteousness. It was the managements duty to carry the orders of the Gurus to each home. But the committees have forgotten their responsibility and are running after titles and treasuries and wasting their energy.

Gurdwaras are meant for meditation. This is the place where subject of opening our Tenth Door to clear vision was to be taught there. I want to tell you that you cannot get salvation by merely bowing your heads. The Guru says, "You cannot get salvation merely by looking at the Guru until you ponder his teachings." The Guru further says, "What will happen by merely bowing your heads when your mind is impure?" Therefore remove corruption from your minds. You all go to the Gurdwaras to bow your heads but you do not act upon the commandments that are given there.

Stop giving useless speeches and empty lectures. Look inside your minds. When your minds are purified, then there will be progress in your states and in your country; improvement will come by itself. The scripture says, "Everybody commits mistakes, only the Guru and God do not err." God is looking at what you are doing. One day you will have to give your explanation in His court. It is written in the Guru Granth Sahib, "You will go naked to hell and appear very frightful!" No one will save you there. You will be thrown into the fire of hell. Your form will become frightful to see. An inquiry will be made into all your actions. Therefore, see the Creator in the Creation.

Your preaching is quite different from what your actions. You are attacking others but you are making the same mistakes that you do not want others to commit. The Guru is always watching you and is always present. Gurbani (Sikh scripture) says, "My Guru is omnipresent; he neither comes nor goes. He is immortal and pervades every particle. When You are forgotten, I am beset by all the evils. When You come in my heart, only then can I serve." When the Guru is with you, then there will be no evil, no corruption. Model your life after our great Sikh ancestors. Become like those who possessed will power, love, and a willingness to sacrifice. At present your life is like the passage of scripture: "Neither are you listening to God's praises nor are you praising God. You are merely making the sky fall by talking."

Let us now obey the commandments of the Gurus, because you will only be accepted when you obey the commandments. Once you obey the commands, prosperity and success will follow you. The Guru has promised that when you forsake your own selfish thoughts and follow the Guru's instructions, society itself will be improved. By following the Guru's instructions, your minds will also be transformed. You will see the presence of God in everything.

Responsible people should go to every village and every home and convey the commandments of God. Direct the energy of your mind toward good. Why collect false wealth? It will not accompany you. There is no need to create parties. Join the party of the One God. What is the use of separate parties? We should do that work that has been given to us by the Guru. Why are you wasting time?

The Gurus converted the lives of tyrants. Greedy people like Malik Bhago were transformed into philanthropists. Our seers themselves were worshipping God and also teaching goodness. They were giving the same instructions to all: "Everyone is part of y community – no one is an outsider" Think of doing good to all. Do whatever the Guru teaches. The Guru speaks of taking care of the burning world: "Oh God, through whichever please save them."

Why are you wasting your precious lifetime making separate parties? I will appeal to you all and to the whole world that human beings should follow their respective chosen prophets or deities; Stop your lectures that criticize and create mutual enmities. Do not waste time. Rise early in the morning, recite God's Holy Name, meditate, and emphasize recognizing the Source of enlightenment.

The scripture says, "Human life is rare; one cannot get it again. Kali Yuga is best of all ages, for one can be saved simply by chanting God's Holy Name." Make use of this time. Do not waste it. As the Guru Granth Sahib says, "Whom should we call good or bad? All are His creatures." Pray for the good of all and make your world and the next world comfortable.

Duties of the Ruler

To the then Prime Minister of India, Sh. P.V. Narasimha Rao, to whom Babaji presented the Guru Granth Sahib in Hindi

A person's fame develops according to his dharam. A person attains power to strengthen law and order, to strengthen the country, to strengthen the people. But if there is no dharam, neither the country nor the people will be strong.

In our country, two things are always linked: dharam and policy. Why are good policies to be adopted and dharam upheld? So that justice will arise; so that people will have the willpower to be just. If there is corruption, the dharmic person will say, "Stop it!" Dharam imparts very strong willpower. The real sense of dharam is not using power for personal ends, but using it strongly for the benefit of the country.

In our country we have different castes, different high classes, different low classes. If we end all these distinctions today, our country will have no equal in the world. These distinctions are obstacles: caste stands before you, upper class stands before you, lower class stands before you. By contrast, look at what occurs in dharam. Look at the Guru Granth Sahib, for instance. There is no low caste, no community which has not been included in it. We cannot call it sectarian religion. It is dharam. Guru Nanak said, "If you are to believe in God, leave these small pathways. Talk about the big highways." What is the highway? To recognize, "I am a human being and you are also a human being. There is no difference between your character and my character. You respect me. If my character is low, then do not respect me. Who are we to respect? Those of high character."

Two things should always be controlled: Maintain law and order, and never use religion for your own purposes. Dharam is an inner matter. If you become a ruler, dharam will tell you, "Oh ruler, be truthful, generous, and cool-tempered. Be kind and just to the people."

What is the greatest way to worship? Being compassionate towards the people, thinking of the development of the country, and doing justice. Guru Nanak says these are the duties of the ruler. As Lord Krishna says, "One who is cruel, one who sees cruelty, and one who tolerates cruelty are all the same." Whenever you see cruelty, challenge it. Whenever you see corruption, challenge it.

Wherever the Guru Granth Sahib goes, light goes. Its greatest quality is that all the bhagats (devotional saints) are sitting within it. When we bow our head before it, we are bowing before the whole Creation.

In Guru Granth Sahib, Guru Nanak emphasized that one who believes in castes and divides the prophets into sects is the enemy of God. Now there is just one thing to be done in our country: We should give up the caste system, and recognize that a person who misuses dharam is against dharam and against society. Dharam is not to be used for personal gain. Dharam is for maintaining law and order. Now we are using dharam for our own ends.

On this subject Guru Gobind Singh once said, "The temple and mosque are the same, puja and namaz are the same ... The Provider and the Merciful One are the same, the Creator and the Benevolent One are the same." He said," All things are His. If puja is being performed, sit there. If namaz is being offered, sit there. If kirtan is being sung, sit there. All are in praise of God."

The Prime Minister is standing here. He has a great responsibility to see that whenever decisions are made, they are made on the basis of a person's merit, his loyalty to the country, the struggles he has faced, and the good deeds he has done. Medals should be awarded for those qualities and decisions taken on this basis alone. Decisions should never be made on the basis of caste. When a decision is based on caste, there will be rebellion in the country. Man has made this caste system. God has not made it.

I will say to you all – the dehra walas, the rulers, the kirtan walas – that Guru Sahib has strictly prohibited taking offerings for conducting worship or and strictly prohibited being worshipped oneself. I am not speaking to you as a guru or pir. I am a working man. I work the whole day, and whatever we produce we distribute among all. Why? I do not believe in being a guru, prophet, or *aulia* (Muslim saint). I always pray to God that I should become a good person, that I should worship the feet of a good man.

May God bless these leaders. As our country is flourishing, we are proud of it. As our country is progressing, we are proud of it. Before, our people did not have anything. Now in the villages they have good cottages. Why? Great development has occurred, indescribable progress …

The Guru Granth Sahib is going, and wherever it goes, it will bestow light, light, light.

SEEK THE WELLBEING OF EVERYONE

To the Governor of the north Indian state of Haryana

Corruption is the greatest evil. It is as bad as poison, for it takes away the rights of others. We should focus on how to abolish it, how to abolish crime, how to bring peace to our country, how to uplift a good person, and how to bring down a bad person. If we do so, our country and our state will become great.

Dharam always tells us, "Be compassionate. Act justly. Speak truth. Be loving. Serve gladly. Seek the wellbeing of everyone.

A person in whom, dharam has developed will seek the wellbeing of everyone, for he will be without enmity. He will want to see everyone smiling, making a good living, having good clothing, living in a good house.

But how are people to attain those good things? Not with corruption. Instead, with our own good resources, good management, observance of law and order. The more law and order prevails, the more the country will progress. And to the extent that dharam is strong in a country, law and order will also be strong.

Religion is not separate from life. Dharam is within everyone. Love itself is within everyone. Compassion itself is within everyone. Truth itself is within everyone. But we have to consider which qualities we should develop. Everything is within us.

What is the best course for us at present? With whatever energy we have, whatever power we have, whatever blessings we can take from God for action, we should stress only one thing: Remove all caste distinctions and serve everyone as one human being to another human being. See everyone as fellow human beings, do justice by considering a person a fellow human being, and love a person as a fellow human being. Then our difficulties will continually diminish.

A person creates difficulties for himself. There is nothing difficult. If we look at it, the same God that is within me is within you. The same truth that is within me is within you. Our subjects are a bit different, but nothing else.

One person believes that God exists; the other questions whether God exists or not. Therein lies the difference. One person maintains that by worshipping, one attains the truth. The other says that so-and-so worships but still takes bribes. But worship does not tell you to be corrupt. Even though people may be behaving badly, religion teaches that we should not be corrupt.

Remember this: Opportunities always come, periods come and go, every season has its time. What is the time now? Time to have faith in religion, faith in people, faith in your country, faith in your office, and faith in your state. No matter how much work we do now, we should do ten times more than that. Then what will happen? People will change, our states will change, and our country will change.

If we do not pray, it is very difficult to bear our karmas (the fruits of our actions). But karma can be changed so quickly that in the twinkling of an eye nothing is left of it. I see people coming here very worried, under great pressure. I give a person Jaap Sahib to read and tell him to pray. When he comes the next time, he comes in a happy mood, saying, "That problem is solved." We say, "Your karma was disturbing you. Now your bad karma has been burned away and your good karma has developed. Now you are happy because that darkness has been removed and the light has manifested within you."

In fact, we all have light within ourselves. My wish for all of you is that you will awaken that light today. And always be happy – laugh, play, and progress. Worry only when you have hurt somebody. Keep working. You will see that if we keep working, keep loving God, our way will be cleared. If we have seen a person as our enemy, perhaps he will become a friend. Whereas we had felt that he was a great obstruction, it is possible that he will become our friend, stand beside us, and move alongside us. Why? Because

God dwells within everyone. He will make a person stand and tell him, "He is your friend, and you are his friend."

God is not our creation. God exists. He is the King of the Spirit. When we love Him, all of Creation will love us. He changes karmas instantly. His nature is very merciful. He does not look at a person's faults. If He looked at the mistakes we make throughout the day, no one would be spared. But He is blessing us twenty-four hours a day, because this is His mission.

How Does Dharam Spread?

To visiting government officials before Gobind Sadan's celebration of Guru Nanak's birthday

Dharam has chiefly been spread either by those in positions of secular power, or by those who go out and serve the people directly. If the powers that be, such as scientists or political figures, turn their attention to dharam and help to develop society, and provide financial support, when those at the bottom see this, their hearts will automatically be touched. They will say, "Aha – so there is kindness in religion? Is this what religion is? Look: That person was very poor and they came and sat with him. Those people had no clothes, and these religious people tried to provide for their needs. They are concerned about our education; they have built schools. They are satisfying our worldly needs and saying that all this has come by God's grace." Worldly self-interest can always be satisfied by worldly powers; the people see what has been done and they move in that direction. One can thus spread dharam through the use of political power.

Throughout history, there have been those who go out among the ignorant people with little understanding. They talk with them, deepen their understanding, help to develop their minds and raise their standards. Some people will follow them with conviction, feeling, "If dharam does this for us, it is very good thing." If worldly help and educational uplift are combined, dharam will spread widely.

However, typically the people with political power are loathe to refer to God in their political setting. They have a negative view of those who preach religion, for they see that those who have set themselves up as authorities do not give anyone good advice, do not help anyone, and do not speak with kindness. That is not religion.

Whenever any religion spreads, perhaps through building schools or hospitals, or through going among the people to help them understand, that is a sacrifice. If you could be enjoying yourself on vacation, but instead give that time to others, taking your ideas into ignorant society, this is a very great sacrifice.

Why hasn't the religion of India spread? This is the place where the Vedas were created, so long ago that we don't even know their age. The Vedas are full of science, full of meditation, full of enlightenment. Then great messengers of God came forth in India, speaking about meditation.

Buddha was born here, and his religion did spread beyond India, because the Indian King Ashoka followed Buddha's teachings and his whole family preached the message of Buddha in other countries. Ashoka combined the worldly kingdom with dharam, and then preached non-violence, and the message spread outward.

The discipline of love

Why did the teachings of Jesus spread? His disciples didn't confine themselves to particulars. They only spoke of love, truth, faith, and service. Jesus emphasized, "Love my Father. God is truth, God is love. Have faith in Him. He will always give you His healing, His blessings, His love." He didn't preach about how to eat, how to drink, how to sleep. He said, "Don't tell lies, don't commit crimes, don't hurt anyone's feelings, don't get angry, don't judge anybody. Keep your thoughts clean. If your thoughts are clean, they will never turn toward evil." Similarly, Guru Gobind Singh said, "Listen all of you, for I speak the truth: Only those who have loved God have realized God."

Religion has not spread from India because our religious spokespeople have created boundaries, and because one person tells lies, another takes bribes, another denies people's rights, and another has no character. Our Indian preachers lecture others not to drink liquor or eat meat, but they themselves are in the habit of eating meat and drinking. All day long they say that liquor is bad, and at night they drink a whole bottle. In other countries, religious figures do not make themselves authorities over such matters. They have the desire to serve; they give love first.

If you love someone, you will do whatever they want. You won't do what they don't want. When you sit together as friends, you know what the desires of your friend are. Therefore, first teach people to love God. Then they will do as God wants. Instead, people are preaching instructions which others are not ready to hear, so dharam does not spread.

If your boss is coming to your house, you consider every detail of what pleases him. Perhaps he likes roses, pictures of nature, good books. You put those near where he will sit. You put out a small spoon for him because you know he takes small bites. You give him a straight chair rather than an easy chair, for you know this is his preference. You go to so much trouble to please your boss that you change the whole environment in your house. Why? Because you will receive something from him.

If we fall in love with God, we will automatically improve everything in our lives, for we want to do what He wants. God says, "Don't lie," so we won't lie. If God says, "Don't eat meat," we won't eat meat. If God says, "Don't drink liquor," we won't drink. If God says, "Wear special clothes," we will wear them. If God says, "Sleep like this," we will sleep like that. What God wants becomes the inner desire of our conscience.

Guru Nanak said, "You are quarreling about eating meat, but you don't understand enlightened wisdom." We tell people, "Don't eat meat," but we don't understand what it is. Actually, we take in minute beings as we breathe. There are bacteria throughout our body. We are born of flesh, in our mother's wombs, and nursed from flesh at our mother's breast. There is life in a lentil, or it would not sprout. Actually, no one is a complete vegetarian. Guru Nanak said, "Everything has life, and yet you are arguing about these things. Tell people about meditation. Tell them about enlightenment." But the ignorant priests didn't understand. They were standing in the dark, and they took teachings that came from enlightened vision and kept them in the dark.

If you look deeply, Guru Nanak also taught the same message that Jesus preached. But we have understood that Guru Nanak's way is different. We started to preach things which are unnecessary.

I think, Oh Master, you gave us so much enlightened wisdom; how will the people understand? These people are ignorant. They are used to living in the dark, whereas You are saying, "Come into the light." When people are in the habit of living and sleeping in the dark, when they come out into the light, they blink and cannot see. When we come from the darkness into the light of truth, we also blink.

To look at the sun, you have to be like a sun yourself. The sun is always giving light, and wherever its rays fall, all things flourish and diseases are eliminated. Without the sun's light, the world would end. God, the Creator of the sun, is also like a Light, giving light to everything.

It is very important for the person who speaks about religion to have an enlightened understanding of religion. If he has no understand, he himself is standing in a dark pit and he is telling others to jump in with him.

Guru Nanak always talked about enlightened wisdom. Science was within his knowledge, and inner vision, and the existence of God. But today officers and managers are afraid to take the name of religion. Oh people, why don't you take the name of the Light? When the light will come, you will surely blink at first, but then you will become accustomed to living in the light.

It is very important for us to follow religion, to be connected to love, to understand God. But people don't understand this. We should record everything which is spoken from enlightenment, for that which is born of enlightenment will create enlightenment. That which is spoken from thoughts will develop your thoughts, but enlightenment is a very great power. With enlightened vision, a person becomes a dervish, a caliph, or one of the Five Beloveds of Guru Gobind Singh. With enlightenment, people sacrifice their lives. When enlightened people speak, others are transformed.

Dharam is very advanced

It is unfortunate that scientists and dervishes never sit together, for they do not understand each other's language. If only they would sit together, they would understand each other. The scientist is considered an atheist, but it is just that he meditates in a different way from the saint. The scientist's meditation is to research everything, to keep studying everything. He is focusing his mind, and that is also meditation.

Scientists try to explain the essential principles of life. When matters extend beyond the limits of their understanding, the best scientists will say, "There is something beyond this." They do not say, "We have researched this subject till the end." They say, "Beyond our research, there is something else." The scientist will start to search for That, but will find that it is very difficult to discover. He or she will then admit, "Science is a very great discipline, but I could only reach this result. There is more beyond."

Similarly, the dervish says, "God showed me so much, but there is even more to the Creation of the Creator." Both the scientist and dervish are meditating, each in their own way. Both have focused their minds and are utterly absorbed in their subject. The scientist is trying to understand the essential principles of things, and the dervish is talking with their Creator.

Look at Guru Nanak. As he sat in meditation, he said, "There are millions of planets, millions of galaxies, worlds upon worlds." Scientists also conclude from their research that many planetary bodies exist; the dervish uses enlightened vision to see the same thing.

Advanced science has only recently proved what was revealed long ago by the dervishes and prophets. Scientists are now able to take pictures of the planets from space, and look how much money it costs to transmit them back to earth. One space probe mission may not be enough; they may have to go five or ten times, and then countries may come to the conclusion that a joint project is necessary.

The dervish is just sitting there alone in his hut. He doesn't even have a penny. He has nothing. He sits there and says, "There are millions and millions of planets, millions of suns." He doesn't need to create multinational projects or solicit any funding. He focuses his vision on the Creator and keeps looking and then writing, looking and then writing.

It is very important for people to understand that what has been accepted as science has already been written about in dharam. What the scientists have researched has not been studied by the common people, and yet scientific conclusions are today accepted in all countries. Dharam is not so universally accepted, so it is very important to the record: Dharam is very advanced. Dharam is very advanced in science, in enlightenment, in peace, and in love. The dervish takes no pride in what he says, so dharam is also advanced in this respect. Whatever the dervish does, he or she says that God has done it.

The dervish said long ago that the earth is round and that the sky stands without pillars. He said that the planets maintain their orbits and their distance from the earth because of gravity. God told him, and so he said, that their speed had to remain constant or they would collide. He said that a small piece of intergalactic material fell to earth, and the earth's orbit expanded.

It is important for dharam to spread all over the world. But what can we do? Where are the people who spread religion? Often I say, Oh, Guru Nanak, you have told us so much about science, you have given us so much enlightened wisdom. You have told us how people are conceived, and by which route people leave this life. You haven't left out anything. But after that, no one has done anything. They have put everything in storage, and the doors to the store room are all rusty. The store room itself is mouldy, and even the locks are rusted.

Guru Nanak spoke of such profound things. If people were to recognize this, they would be amazed by the depth to which he went. But everything has its own time. Night has to come, and after that, day will follow. Both bad times and good times have to come. This has always been the rule: how long shall darkness and clouds obscure the sun? One hour, two hours? At the end, there will be so much brilliance. The sun will set aside all darkness as it rises. God's Light is ever-powerful.

Sharing his message of God's love and peace with all people

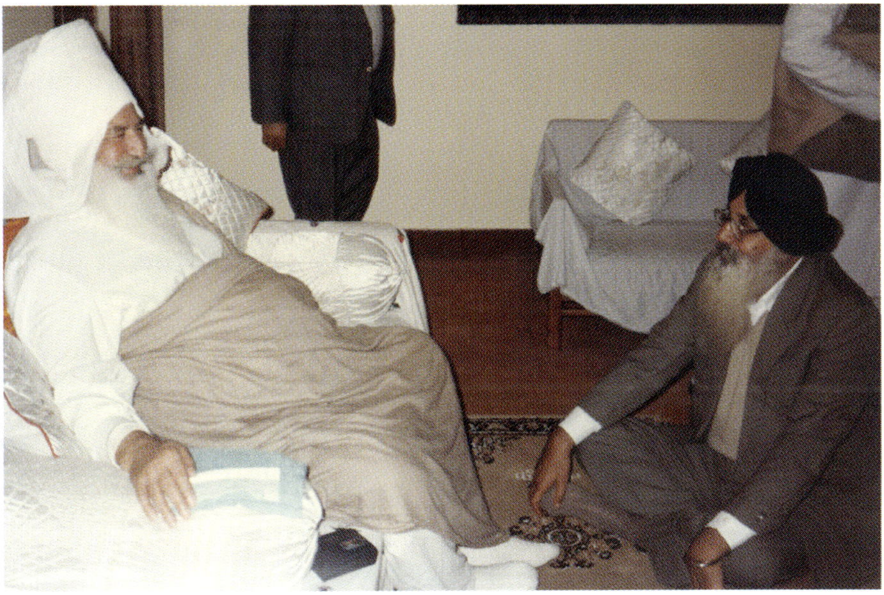

From Chief Minister to Prime Minister
S. Parkash Singh Badal, Chief Minister Punjab

Presenting Guru Granth Sahib in Hindi to Prime Minister Narasima Rao,
(S. Buta Singh, Home Minister, in the middle)

From the poor farmer to the leading intellectuals
Talking with villagers in Shiv Sadan, with Gurdev Singh and Balwant Singh

With delegates to International Forum on Enlightened Development
at Gobind Sadan (2007)

From the dais in India First Jaap Sahib Seminar, Gobind Sadan – Dr. S. A. Ali, Surendra Nath, Babaji, Father Mark, Swaranjit Singh, (1990)

Release of Jaap Sahib translation at Indian Int'l Center (1992)

Stage at Forum on Enlightened Development, Gobind Sadan Auditorium (2007)

Healing Russia

Blessing the children at Snegiri, May 2004

Welcomed by Moscow Mayor, Yuriy Luschkov, Luschkov's Office, May 2004

Members of Peace through Culture surround Babaji on their first visit to Gobind Sadan (1998)

One Good Person can make a Difference

To an official who asked Babaji's blessings for his dream of eradicating the corruption that pervades Indian society

People have developed the attitude and it has become so entrenched in their minds, that it makes no difference if you hurt another's feelings or accept bribes. Training in dharam has declined to such an extent that the world remembers only one thing: self-interest. Everyone can be bought.

Individuals who want to change this are discouraged. They feel, "What can I do by myself ?" But from time immemorial, it has always been just one good person who uplifted his ideals, prayed for God's help, and thus changed the direction of workplaces, of whole countries. Why has a single person been successful in this? Because he speaks with love, from his heart.

Consider the story of Abraham Lincoln. He was a simple woodcutter, at a time when there was a movement to free the African slaves. He was just a poor man, but he thought to himself, "Have I just taken birth to sell wood or have I come here for some other purpose? What can I do to help these people?" He was only one person, with no organization. But he began speaking to people of the injustice of slavery. In his determination to help the slaves, he began learning to read the alphabet, and eventually began speaking on behalf of the slaves in court. When he ran for election and was defeated, he said, "My mind is not defeated. My mind has become stronger through this defeat." Eventually this small farmer became the top lawmaker of the United States.

Truth is never in the majority. It is not a matter of quantity – its strength lies in quality. The majority are like sheep. If you catch hold of one sheep, all the others will follow bleating.

It is my firm belief that when a person sets a goal and puts his energy into achieving it, he will never be disappointed. When you set a good goal, God will help you one hundred percent – not ninety percent. God will bring out His people and tell them: Let us go where there is a goal.

If you mention your goal to someone else, he will say, "What can you alone do?" But God is only One; God is not two. A saint is only one. The prophet of God is only one, not many. A leader is only one; there are not five or seven leaders. When they make their aim, they rise like the sun. By the grace of God, one person alone carries out scientific research, one person alone changes countries, one person alone changes societies.

It is likely that God is not happy with the state of the world. God works through human beings; God does not work through the air. God raises a person and says, "Oh my son, my daughter, Go and tell the world." So the person speaks, go and work there, and God changes the people's minds.

Make this your aim and think of it day and night: "This is our birthplace. We have to make it great. We have to eradicate corruption in this country. We have to bring goodness forth in the people. We have to reestablish the great ancient glory of this country." If bad people have come in, remove them quietly, because a thief has a weak foundation. A thief has great fear in his mind. If there is a little knock at the door, he starts trembling, because he has entered the room in order to steal. A little knock at the door will make the thieves run away.

But always remember: Whatever you want to say, first practice it yourself. Prove that you yourself will not practice corruption, that you can not be bought. It is not necessary to make a big commotion. The point is to strengthen your character. Truthfulness is not a matter of talking; it is a matter of action. When they see that you do not practice corruption and that there is so much progress in your department, everyone's thinking will be changed. Those who will rise against you have no goal. Their arrows will be wasted. You have the goal, and your arrows will strike them.

A person's glory diminishes when he is unjust, when he deprives others of their rights. The end of this cycle of bad people is approaching. God is watching. God knows. As Guru Gobind Singh said, "Do not trouble Creation, because it belongs to the Creator. When Creation is hurt, the Creator becomes angry."

You should not worry. Always remember the One who has created the whole Creation. Do whatever you can for others, from the core of your heart. Your glory will increase and the things you do not want will decrease. This is the eternal nature of God. Today people think they will become great through money, but no! One becomes great through high principles, through progressive ideas, through serving people, through loving people.

Do not be overwhelmed by today's situation. It will not last very long. It is just a drama.

Ending Terrorism

A message after September 11, 2001

What is terrorism? It is just an idea. It's a matter of which direction one develops one's thoughts. By developing an idea one can become a great prophet or a brave warrior, commit crimes or begin killing people. Ideas can never be ended by war. We must explain to people, giving examples and interacting with them.

There is no society, no country, no place called "terrorism." It is just an idea that has developed. Throughout the ages, prophets have come to change the way we think. The Messiah, the Nabi, the Gurus have all come for the same purpose: to promote good ideas and put an end to bad ideas. Trying to respond to war through war will only create more negative thoughts.

A new wave has begun which we call terrorism. Without proper understanding, this wave cannot be stopped. It will be stopped only if religion transforms people's minds, and that will happen only if religion is guided by enlightenment. Through enlightenment, bad actions will be eliminated and good actions will develop. If we do not change, there was no need for the prophets to come and sacrifice so much. The whole reason they came was to transform our minds through their struggles, meditation, and sacrifices.

Today this sickness of terrorism has spread all over, but it is not new in India. Nearly a thousand years ago our sisters, daughters and property were being carried away by invaders. We believed that it was the duty of the king to save our daughters, to protect our property and our homes. But during those times, the rulers lost control, and the society could not protect itself. After centuries of this terrorism, Guru Nanak came with words of love, with the power of healing and meditation. He raised his voice against this injustice and explained that sitting in worship does not mean that you should allow someone to snatch your property, your home, your daughters. Very lovingly he taught that if you cannot protect your honour, your worship is useless. True worship means that "If you recite the Name of the Fearless One, fear will vanish." When a person truly worships God, he becomes fearless and without enmity. Then a person who meditates will save not only his own daughters but also others' daughters and protect others' property.

Guru Nanak's voice was very powerful, and it spread. But the invaders' voices were also very strong because they had become addicted to stealing and brutal killing. Finally when Guru Gobind Singh came, he instilled his healing power into the Panj Piaras (the first five Khalsa initiates) made them very brave, and trained them. So much power and healing came from their voice that other people changed. They overcame their fear and began to protect every home, every community; they took responsibility for the whole country. If anyone invaded the country, the Khalsa at once confronted them bravely, disarmed them, rescued the women, recovered the stolen property, and drove them away.

According to Guru Gobind Singh's teachings, religion is not a sect or a fortress. Neither he nor his followers were in any danger. It was the people who wore the holy thread and applied a sacred mark to their foreheads (Hindus) who were being terrorized. But the Guru created the Khalsa to protect everyone. There were many struggles during that period, and terrorism was removed from our country. This was made possible through their sacrifices, and through loving discourses. For one thing, they inspired fear in the invaders—fear that our people were as brave and powerful as they, that their terrorism would not be tolerated and would be punished, and that they would not be successful in abducting women from our country. They never dared to invade again. Secondly, Guru Nanak travelled to their countries, sat among them, and began to change their minds through his preaching. The atmosphere changed so much that those who had been terrorizing our country's people instead settled here to work for a living. This is the way to uproot terrorism: to create fear in the attackers and at the same time, develop dharam within them.

Today the policy has been adopted to destroy any country labeled as terrorist. What will be the result? One day the country that destroys other countries will be seen as the greater terrorist. Then it cannot say that it is fighting terrorism, for by fighting, that country itself becomes terrorist. The need of the day is to introduce dharam, to develop good policies, and then to uproot terrorism by understanding their problems. They obviously have some difficulties and grievances, and that is why they are killing people. There must be a reason why a person becomes defiant and attacks, why a person commits suicide. Dharam will remove those destructive thoughts.

I become very sad when I think of all those innocent people who died. How long it had taken to bring them up. First they were infants in their mothers' wombs. As they grew up they were educated, nourished, cared for, protected from accidents. Then for them to be killed like that when they were grown is very sad. God will never be happy with that.

We must bear two things in mind: We must take God's blessings, and we must also uproot terrorism. We will receive blessings only if we do not adopt their methods. If we use the same means, then we are the bigger terrorists. Neither God, nor writers, nor history will ever forgive us.

I can speak with authority on this subject because terrorism was widespread in our country. In a single raid, 50,000 women were abducted and 100,000 people killed. Imagine the chaos and the cries that must have filled the air. There must have been terror all around, but even then the response was not cruel. The invaders were helped to understand by love and enlightenment. At that time, there were no modern armaments. They fought on horseback with swords. The invaders had many brave warriors. They always issued a challenge, and then they attacked. But the invaders' movement was wrong, absolutely wrong. The Khalsa instilled fear in the invaders, but also gave them jobs without any feeling of vengeance.

Once a person gets pricked by a thorn on a particular path, he will avoid that path in the future. Catch those who are committing atrocities and offer opportunities to the others. Arrange jobs for them, food, shelter, education for their children, and help them get settled in marriage. When they become busy in their duties, their minds will be busy. How can they then commit terrorism? An idle mind is Satan's workshop. Keep them busy. Satanic thoughts will leave, and healing thoughts will remain.

The great struggles of Guru Gobind Singh's Khalsa were against terrorism, not against any religion. If we had been opposed to Islam, the Guru would not have asked the great Muslim saint Mian Mir to lay the foundation stone of the Golden Temple, nor would the Muslim saint Buddhu Shah have given his sons, his brother, and seven hundred followers in support of the Guru. Islam must not be confused with terrorism. Islam is the teachings of the Prophet Muhammad – teachings of love and compassion.

The teachings of Jesus are those of love and mercy; they have no connection with terrorism. According to his teachings, we cannot go to war. Jesus says, "If someone takes your shirt, give him your coat as well."

It is essential throughout the world, in every religion, to develop good preachers and good people. In every home, people should be taught in depth what are the true teachings of Islam, of Christianity, of Judaism, of Sikhism, and so on. Thus harmony will arise.

Nowadays so many weapons are being made. For what? To kill people. Countries are facing poverty, but still we are manufacturing armaments worth billions of dollars. Listen: Heal the mind that has gone astray. Explain to it, and the mind will understand. In your home, if a child goes wrong, then the mother keeps showering him with love, and he begins to follow her. The father keeps giving him advice, and the child learns.

When our country fell prey to terrorism, how did we eradicate it? We did not destroy any village or kill any innocent people. We just made them leave out of fear, and at the same time, Guru Nanak taught them through enlightenment.

At present it is essential to emphasize and spread good thoughts. Pray with love, asking the Almighty to change their minds, give them enlightenment, and bless their souls. They have gone astray. Not only they – today we are all confused. When a person slips and falls he hurts himself physically. But imagine a person whose mind is slipping all the time – what will his condition be? At present, everyone's mind is slipping. Every person's mind is out of control. Everyone is angry, selfish. Any person who has his eye on another's spouse or property has no base. That person is finished. Change your thoughts. Why should it even enter your mind whether a person is a man or a woman?

In ashrams, in offices, in society, people's minds have slipped. Anyone who does not control his mind will commit corruption, will look lustfully at other people's sisters and daughters, will hurt other people's feelings. The most important question is how to get the mind back into its abode. Your mind will be controlled only when you pay attention to the message of your prophet. Every country has had its prophets. Learn from them, take their enlightened wisdom, and control your minds. Once your minds change, there will be no frustration or anger, for within every person there is the love and healing that Guru Gobind Singh brought forth.

Nowadays there is not only one kind of terrorism. Every office has become terrorist. The person who commits corruption can be viewed as a terrorist; he who deprives others of their rights is a terrorist. A terrorist cannot be recognized because he wears a feather in his cap. The corrupt person is a terrorist. He who attacks another person's religion is also a terrorist. Terrorists do not have horns on their head – it is just that their thoughts are not under their control. Therefore do not fight this act of anger by retaliating in anger.

We have established courts to punish people according to their crimes. Do not just kill them. Killing will not solve the problem, because the person who is killed will be someone's relative and someone's friend – and thus ten more terrorists will spring up in their place. Today the feeling is, "That country which nurtures terrorism should be destroyed." But with this destruction there will be further anger, and that anger will lead to more terrorism. It is possible that a whole country may become terrorist.

Those committing terrorist acts should be caught by any means possible, and then tried and punished according to law. It is essential that those who commit atrocities should be punished. Both worldly law and God's law provide for this. But in order to punish one person you should not destroy ten thousand more. To do so is viewed as a very great crime in God's house. Seeing one person punished, others learn that cruelty will be severely punished, and they will then become afraid to commit cruelty. Do not fight terrorism in such a way that the criminals escape and many innocent people die.

Guru Nanak and Guru Gobind Singh emphasized that to stop terrorism you should keep your character intact, keep your religion intact, keep your morals and goals intact, think of a woman as your sister, your daughter, or your mother, and consider another person's money as poison. At that time our character had become so powerful that our people could not be misled.

We should not fight anger with anger; we should reply with love, and lovingly explain with examples. Not every person is enlightened. We open schools, colleges, and universities to give training and produce great philosophers, scientists, doctors, and prophets, whose training is meditation. These institutions are built to change bad thoughts. No one is born a doctor, a scientist, or a saint. One must be trained.

Today we have labeled those whose minds have gone astray "terrorist." They are consumed with anger and attack with a bomb, not recognizing how many people they will kill. We must control this. Those people should understand, "If someone does the same to you, how will you feel? Now you yourself cannot escape. Take the protection, love, and healing of religion, and control your anger."

I have firm faith that if we hold several meetings of all concerned parties, they will definitely come to an agreement. A human being is not made of stone. A person becomes flexible. A person changes. By a worldly approach, we cannot reach a conclusion in one or two meetings, because one side will ask something and the other side will say, "No." But if you will talk lovingly, they will agree. If you bring in God's grace, they will agree. No one wants to die. No one wants to stay hidden all his life. Everyone wants to be free. They are slaves of their thoughts. Just correct their thoughts. It is not a big thing.

In my life I have seen people change. Many influential people come here. Some do not believe in God, but when we sit with them and explain to them, after some time they are so overcome with love that they begin to meditate, to pray, to praise God, and to criticize evil – even though they themselves may have been doing those same wrong actions before coming here.

When we went to Russia in 1989, Russians were all said to be atheists, but now thousands of them are reading Jaap Sahib, Guru Gobind Singh's divine praises of God. In 1977, when the northeastern Indian state of Mizoram was in chaos from a deadly insurgency movement, we spent three months there, gained the confidence of the terrorists, and also met with the government leaders. A compromise was worked out, and the terrorists laid down their arms. An officer wept at the news, telling us, "I am amazed that religion can correct people's minds. We thought that religion is ineffective."

I am not trying to pass an order as a guru. "Guru" is such a great word that when I hear it, I am immediately reminded of Jesus, who was crucified. I am reminded of the Sahib zadas, the four sons of Guru Gobind Singh who were martyred. Truth always faces retaliation. When someone speaks truth, people stand up to oppose him and ask, "Who are you to speak this way?"

You may question why I am advising not to destroy that country. It is my feeling, my thought, my vision that this problem will be solved not by killing but by love. The sword should not be answered with the sword. Explain to them; they may lay down their swords. Explain to them, and perhaps their minds will be changed. Terrorism has sprouted from pressure; it will not be ended by pressure.

You must keep in mind that the anger that has arisen within you may result in a world war. When you will destroy any country, another country will stand by its side. When one is being beaten, another will stand by him in sympathy. Do not answer their anger with anger. They are not animals who will not understand. They are human beings like us. They have the same ears, same eyes, same body as we. The only difference is that bad thoughts have entered their minds. Bad thoughts can also occur in us. Thoughts can be transformed to good thoughts and used in a positive direction.

Today there is anger in every home. Our children are filled with anger. There are fights in our homes, divorces in our homes. Why? Because our thoughts are not under control. Our children go astray because their thoughts are not under control. You would not think of killing those children. They must instead be controlled.

Those whom we call terrorists are like children gone astray, because they have been misguided. Their ideas have been developed in the wrong direction: "How can we destroy this building? How many people can be killed in this building?" There could instead be another line of thinking: "We are to make a building – how is it to be built to protect us from rain and thunder?" How would the latter thought develop? From good training, good healing.

Anyone can become angry. What is difficult is to bring peace, love, healing. Defiance is easy. It is the duty of us all to control our temper, our corruption, our desire to deprive others of their rights.

We must take the blessings of Guru Gobind Singh, who said, "The God of Hindus and the God of Muslims is the same, temples and mosques are the same." The person trained by Guru Gobind Singh can go into a mosque, a temple, a gurdwara, a church, for he recognizes that God is everywhere. For him or her, there is no boundary. Human beings have created boundaries and think themselves special. He is special in whose heart there is light.

On Violence and Religion

To reporters in Russia

I say here with full conviction, "Until people meditate, peace will never come to the world. Anger destroyed this country and caused tremendous unrest." Here in Russia it is as if someone has been locked in jail for a long time. When the door is finally opened, they run out with great joy. Being told that there is no God, they were locked in a jail. Now they are free to say, "Yes, God exists," and they are all enjoying and celebrating their freedom.

Whenever I talk about meditation, they fall totally in love with the idea and go out and write books about whatever I say and also show it on television. I can see from all these things that they will become very spiritual. Seeing them meditate is something that will change the whole future of the world. I have met people from all walks of life here and as yet, I have not seen anything that would indicate that there is any block to spirituality in this country. Their whole system will turn around and thank God. They will also progress greatly as a country.

I appeal to all countries: If you say that you love God, then follow His orders. If you say, "Jesus is ours," then follow his teachings. Jesus would never accept someone killing another person. If you have been stoned by someone, offer them flowers. If someone throws a stone, we should not shoot them with a machine gun. That makes Jesus very unhappy. Jesus says that if someone is beating you, turn to God and say, "Oh God, please forgive them, forgive them, forgive them. They do not know what they are doing." Forsake war. Take the money that you are spending on war and help those in need. Give them good housing, good food, good education. Make medicines affordable. Do not destroy the progress that you have made in your country. Maintain it. Put the gifts that God has given you to good use. When you hurt somebody's feelings, Jesus becomes very unhappy. When you kill somebody, Jesus becomes very angry. Why should we make Jesus angry?

If you love Moses, follow his teachings and his example. Moses is the greatest example of personal sacrifice to help the weak. He renounced a kingdom to free the slaves. A true follower of Moses can never attack the weak or tolerate tyranny.

If you love Guru Gobind Singh, do as he did. His history is one of standing up for the weak. A true follower of Guru Gobind Singh can never observe any distinctions between high and low. He can never attack anyone's holy place. As Guru Gobind Singh said, "The mosque and the temple are the same; puja and namaz are the same. Recognize all people as one human race."

God is happy with those who are compassionate, not with those who are angry. Love everyone. Love all countries. Help them overcome their weaknesses. If there is poverty, send them medicine. If they have other weaknesses, educate them. Turn that river of wealth in other directions; turn off the supply for war. It is not good for any country. God is not happy, the public will not be happy, and you will not be happy."

Question: Why is there so much terrorism among Muslims? Is it because of their religion?

Babaji: The Holy Qur'an teaches us to love our neighbours, to love everyone. It says to fight for Allah's sake, but what is the jihad of Allah? To rescue anyone who is oppressed, to defend those who are being threatened or hurt. The Holy Qur'an says that a kafir (unbeliever) is one who suppresses the truth, whereas a mu'min (believer) is one who bears witness to the truth. To the Prophet Muhammad, it is not a question of being a Muslim, a Jew, a Sikh, or a Hindu. He is talking about people's virtues. Any Muslim who kills or puts pressure on others is by definition a kafir. And anyone who is kind to others, who thinks how to help others, who always sees the light of God in others is a true mu'min. Anyone who fights from enmity, from jealousy is going against Islam. When we speak of the "jihad of Allah," we mean that one does not fight for one's fame, nor worry about being criticized; nor should the struggle be for the sake of any nation or race but simply to save people from oppression, to make the weak strong, to give power to the poor, no matter what religion they follow. Then you can say that the fight is for Allah.

Many people have become terrorists. One person drops a bomb and blows up an entire city. What could he be called? A terrorist – a big terrorist. Another person sets off a bomb in the market and kills two hundred people, and the newspaper calls him a terrorist. Whether a person comes out of the jungle and throws a bomb or lives in the city and drops bombs from an airplane, both are terrorists. Both sides kill each other, but only one side is labeled terrorist. The press is afraid to challenge the strong so they all go after the weak.

A terrorist is one who kills people, creates fear in people, puts pressure on people, and plunders their resources. A person who takes bribes, who takes away people's rights, who threatens or suppresses people, or who creates laws in his own self-interest is also a terrorist, because he spreads fear. We cannot say that terrorism is being spread only by young people. Somewhere a war is raging. Big artillery guns are being fired and people are being killed. Whole countries are committing terrorism. In one house, someone is dead and the children are crying; this is all terrorism. It spreads fear which is like slow suicide. Somewhere mosques are being destroyed; somewhere temples, churches, or synagogues are being destroyed. Terrorism has cast its shadow over the whole world.

This is not a question of Muslim, Sikh, Hindu, Jewish, or Christian extremism. This kind of conduct is prohibited in every scripture, be it the Bible, the Torah, the Qur'an, the Zend Avesta, or the Guru Granth Sahib. The people who are criticizing terrorism, who are holding meetings to determine how to stop terrorism, should first stop and look within themselves. Are they themselves not committing terrorism? We should first remove the terrorism within ourselves. We should give up anger and desire for revenge, should forsake the idea of bombing countries. Only then will there be peace and cooling in the world. When Babar was terrorizing the people of India, Guru Nanak said, "You are not Babar, you are Zabbar (one who grabs forcibly), you are kafir (non-believer). If a powerful person kills another powerful person, there is no grief in my heart, but you are killing the weak. So I humbly pray to God, 'The people are being beaten so badly; did You not feel any pain?'"

Terrorism is not a matter of one religion; no one is obeying the teachings of their own prophets. If the rulers and influential people in countries will act according to the teachings of their prophets, peace will come automatically.

No One is a Terrorist

To Gobind Sadan Institute's seminar, "Blessed are the Peacemakers: the Spiritual Approach to Peace"

Terrorism arises out of pressure. What I have seen is that nobody is a terrorist and no one is an atheist. Rather, it is misguided teachings that influence their behavior. The way we are approaching the problem we will never get rid of terrorism. With pressure, it will only increase. The more you try to suppress it, the more it will spread.

Now we should first stop and think what terrorism really means. It means to spread fear. By that definition, a corrupt person is also a terrorist. A person who suppresses someone else's voice is also a terrorist; a person who suppresses another's religion is also a terrorist. We must first try to understand what motivates them. Why do they rebel? They must have some difficulties.

The day they come to you, treat them like your family, treat them like you would your own children. If one of our children rebels, we'll think of many ways to bring the child home and try to understand why he is rebelling. But we would never shoot that child. Now someone will stand up and say, "I want to finish terrorism," but such people themselves are terrorists. They are corrupt and filled with anger and greed. When a person is angry, what we know as dharam, as truth and justice, is finished. Today anger has spread throughout the world.

First find out what the people who are rebelling are thinking. Ask, "Why do you do this? Is someone taking away your rights, or is there any other cause?" They will tell you their problem. Then treat that problem. You are doing an operation without knowing what the ailment is. If you operate without a diagnosis, the person will die. Operate according to the confirmed diagnosis. To start shooting is not the way. First learn whether or not it is necessary to shoot. If you were a doctor, you are giving pills for which there is no need; similarly, you are shooting bullets to end terrorism without need. Now people are not asking. They only give orders:

"He is a terrorist, so shoot him."

Today terrorism is not a problem of one village or country – it has spread over the whole world, and the whole world is speaking against it. It is not a simple thing now – it requires great thought. If it were a matter of one village, only one village would be harmed, but now it is a matter of the whole world.

What has come from this word "terrorism"? One country has risen up and attacked so many countries, has destroyed whole countries, saying, "They are terrorists." There are so many other countries like this. Just wait – perhaps some other country may do the same. One country has already done so much harm that we cannot restore what has been destroyed. Thousands and millions of people have been killed in the name of fighting terrorism.

You should look deeply into the matter – Why are people rebelling? Perhaps there has been some injustice or insult. Perhaps their daughter or sister has been insulted, and that is why they are rebelling. When such people give statements, the other type of people think, "They have attacked us." Just as when someone says, "Corruption is a bad thing," all the people who are corrupt think, "He is attacking us." Similarly, those people are fighting whose rights have been taken away. The title given to them is "terrorists," rather than "those who are fighting for their rights." So be very careful about these things. Try to understand what terrorism is. Until you do, terrorism will not end.

Nowadays countries are meeting about terrorism. What do they do in the meetings? One senior person says, "We will end terrorism." But he himself has killed millions of people by bombing them. However, the others will not ask him, "What should we call you?" Because cowardly people are sitting there, and because he is a strong person with so many weapons and so much money, no one will question him. So long as these things are not discussed in the meetings, terrorism will not end. All are cowards.

In our country, invaders used to come and plunder the country's wealth and also take away the young girls. Nobody said anything. They were afraid: "They will kill us if we speak up." The same thing is happening now – people are cowardly like them. To accept cruelty, to see cruelty, and to commit cruelty are the same.

These days, everybody is worrying about their own children, their own interests. No one is concerned about the public. That is why cruelty is growing and law and order is breaking down. Terror is everywhere. It is not just a matter of a person stepping out of the jungle and throwing a bomb; girls are being abducted in the markets, and whole cities and factories are being bombed. No one is representing the public's grief and sorrows. By contrast, Guru Nanak spoke up for the public and worked for the people. He aroused fearlessness in the people. He trained the people to help others, he trained people to earn their righteous livelihood, and he trained them to speak with courage. Guru Gobind Singh also brought the same effects. Thus our country somewhat revived. But now people have forgotten the teaching of sacrifice that was given by the Gurus. That is why in these days there is no law and order; no one is safe. How can a responsible person sleep soundly? One day everyone has to go, but the person who will die doing God's duty will be remembered in the history books. Now people are sleeping, but we must wake them up and bring those things to the surface again. Otherwise, in the name of terrorism, all the world will be destroyed.

Nothing Good Comes From War

Nothing good comes from war. War does not discriminate. It kills good people, peace-loving people, as well as those who are evil. All our prophets have stressed peace.

To remove a few bad people, you will destroy a whole country and perhaps the world. To rid yourself of one bad person, you would kill countless children and parents. Think of the cries of the orphans for their parents. Think of the cries of the parents for their children. There are always bad people in the world. But to remove them you do not need to kill everyone. Innocent people are always killed in greater numbers than the clever ones who are responsible for creating terrorism or rebellion. In any conflict, the trouble-makers are never easily eliminated, whereas the innocent face great sufferings. All conflicts are ultimately settled by negotiations anyway. Why not sit down and resolve the conflict peacefully? Why are you so eager to wage war?

The message for evildoers everywhere is this: Beware of God, for those innocent people whom you are killing for no reason will not only knock at God's door. They will enter that door, and then you will be punished very heavily by the Almighty.

Our ultimate goal should be to spread peace and allow people to live happily. We should enjoy this beautiful Creation of the Creator and let other people enjoy it, too – its beautiful trees, its mountains, its grasses, its fresh air and clean water. We should not blacken it and earn God's anger forever.

VI

Science and the Mystical Experience: The State of The Planet

Dharam is the greatest science. Hundreds, if not thousands of years ago, visionaries revealed to us what scientists are just now heralding today as their latest discovery.

Visions of the Cosmos

From a discussion with Galina Vladimirova, Russian space scientist

Consider the power of enlightened wisdom. The things that science is telling us after years of lengthy research were already revealed by visionaries as they sat comfortably in meditation. They just closed their eyes and described what they saw. They did not have to spend money on research or use battery cell power. They said that humans have many cells within the brain, and once these are developed, you can see everything that is happening above and below.

Our country's religious texts have already told us that some stars are so far away that it will take tens of millions of years for their rays to reach the earth. In meditation, Guru Nanak, the first Sikh Guru, once said, "This sun that you see is not the only sun – there are tens of millions of suns. This moon that you see is not the only moon – there are tens of millions of such bodies."

Now when a scientist reveals the results of his research, we feel that he discovered something very new. Actually, it is very old knowledge. Scientists are simply proving what has already been revealed. What is meditation? It is like concentrating on something, researching into it, until you reach a conclusion. Whether you are conducting scientific research or meditating and having visions, it is all a matter of inner concentration.

The stronger and clearer your thoughts, the more you are able to focus, the better scientist you will become. Likewise, the clearer your mind, the greater your power of concentration, the better dervish you will become. Worry, fear, and pressure should not enter, for they will torture your mind. In reality, what is meditation? It is a defense system that keeps out the bad and develops the good. The clearer a person's mind, the stronger it becomes for researching to great depths.

Both scientists and dervishes are studying the universe. The scientist studies its components; the dervish studies the One Who made them. The dervish says, "Through my enlightened vision I have seen the whole universe. I call it the Creation, for the Creator has produced it." It is as if one person insists that a tree has branches, while another says that the tree has a trunk and speaks of the One who creates the branches. Both are correct. And neither discipline has reached its limits. Scientists have asserted that although they have discovered a great deal, there is more beyond what they have found or done. The dervish also declares, "This field is so vast that I cannot explore it fully." It is our duty to study and explore as much as possible, and to provide this information to the people.

Sometimes the scientist becomes worried and doubt sets in, when the parts of his research do not fit together. At that point, he needs the one with the stores of enlightened knowledge to share this knowledge with him, to clear the obstruction in his mind when his research has come to a standstill, and to help him move ahead. The scientist knows about the elements, but sometimes they may confuse him. Inner spiritual knowledge will never confuse a person.

Unfortunately, though the research of the scientist and the dervish is related, they have never collaborated. If the scientist and the dervish were to get together, human knowledge of the universe would increase. If they truly have a meeting of minds, the scientist will not doubt the knowledge of the dervish, and the dervish will respect the scientist's research. Then the scientist will start believing in God. The dervish already does.

See God in All Creation

To a Russian scientist on methods of spiritual attainment

The Fifth Sikh Guru said there are eighty-four yoga postures used to purify the mind, but even by doing them, one will not necessarily become an enlightened being. If one wants to meet God, there is no method for doing so, except one. Whosoever loves God, God loves him.

Guru Nanak said that there are millions of galaxies, millions of suns, millions of planets. He could see them through clear inner vision. He was not using any posture or any method of meditation. But love is so powerful that when one meditates, one does so with God's blessing.

What is meditation? Guru Gobind Singh said, "I meditated so intensely that my light became one with that great Light of Enlightenment. From two, we became one." Guru Gobind Singh says that the soul is a ray of that greater Enlightenment of God. Teach your soul that it has come from that Ocean. Tell your soul: "Don't just remain a small ray, enter the Ocean of Light."

When the Enlightenment of God awakens inside, you may continue eating food or associating with bad or good people, but that inner concentration will be unaffected. How does one attain enlightenment? It comes by itself. It does not come from preaching or pilgrimage to holy places or temples. It is an inner thing.

I say this because from childhood, I never went to any place of pilgrimage. I never visited any temple or gurdwara or any spiritual person. I was simply sitting in meditation. Great attraction towards Him developed as I sat. As that attraction grew, I used to sing hymns to Him, day and night. I was looking at Him and weeping as I saw Him. I did not meditate by concentrating on my forehead, on this chakra (portal) or that chakra. The One upon Whom we are to meditate said, "Look at Me!"

If anyone asks me, "What is God?" I can say that if from within you have received the enlightenment of your Guru, it is the Truth. Look at a tree, and it will talk to you. Look at the earth, and it will surely talk to you. Why? The One Who has trained you is Master of the whole Creation.

The saint sees the cosmos

It is our misfortune that the scientist and the saint have never sat down together. The scientist thinks the saint is illiterate. He feels, "I am a learned man. Why should I sit with an illiterate person?" For his part, the saint is in his own world. He feels, "The scientist is an atheist. What have I to do with him?" But both are carrying out research. Neither is an atheist. The scientist is carrying out research into the Creation, and the saint is asking, "Where is the Creator who has created this Creation?" The scientist concludes, "Everything develops from genes." The saint says, "It is the work of the Creator. When I went to the Creator, He told me, 'You have seen one sun. You have been meditating on one earth. Now come! Let me show you millions of suns bigger than that one.' I went along with Him, and He showed me many earths, many suns, many moons, millions and millions. Then I said, 'You Yourself understand Your own Power. I have now seen so many celestial bodies. But how can I describe them when I return to earth?' He replied, 'Say only this: That the distance between planets is kharbs of yojans.'" (1 kharb yojan = 250,000,000,000,000 miles)

The Fifth Guru said, "You do not meet Him by working hard or by serving. You meet Him all of a sudden. You may have been developing occult yogic powers and practicing the 84 postures. Thus you will gain long life, but then you will die and have to be born again, and you will not attain union with God."

God is Master of the whole Creation. In describing Him, Guru Gobind Singh said, "God is in water, God is in the earth, God is in caves, God is in mountains, God is here and there. He pervades everything."

The Vedas (ancient scriptures of India) came from Brahma from time immemorial, through the enlightened sages, but those scriptures were lying in a heap, written on palm leaves. Ved Vyas (the great saint) gathered all this knowledge and organized it into four Vedas. What was their essence? To describe God he wrote, "Neti, neti (infinite, infinite). No matter how vast You have appeared, You are beyond that."

Guru Nanak said, "God is One. Accept Him as Truth." The Prophet Muhammad said, "Allah is pure and without equal. Believe in this." Jesus came, calling God "My Father." He said, "My Father is One, King of the Spirit." Guru Gobind Singh likewise said, "When I had communion with God, He said, 'You are My Son. I hand over all My rights to you."

Contemporary science has not yet discovered what Guru Gobind Singh, Guru Nanak and the Vedas were talking about. They said that eventually you may see planets where the people are very beautiful. But the inhabitants may prevent you from reaching there, because they are living in love for each other, in peace, in enlightenment. If you go there, you will surely bring deceit and trouble. How long they can hide from you is uncertain, but they are trying to keep the curtain drawn.

When you see that celestial drama, you question this earthly drama in which we are living. This is just a tiny area in the vastness of the cosmos.

I have never spoken about yogic postures or said, "God resides in this or that part of the body" Where does He live? He lives in all places. When He meets you and speaks with love, the whole Creation will speak to you with love.

God says, "Let it be so!" and it happens

What is God? While I was developing the farms at Shiv Sadan, I've had many opportunities to meet Him in His Creation. Once as we were driving by the fields, Balwant Singh said, "Maharaj, water is pouring into this rice paddy. From your inner vision, please tell us what to do. Should we block the water or not?" I said, "We will ask the rice itself whether it requires water. I believe in God." Immediately the rice appeared in the form of a boxer. He said, "Tell them to let the water come. My muscles will become very strong." I told them not to block the water.

Another time we were traveling by a field in which crops sometimes turned yellow. I said, "We will ask this soil, 'What disease do you have that makes the crops yellow?' " As the answer came to me I had the driver record which nutrients were deficient in this field and what had to be added. "There is an acute Zinc deficiency here," said the earth. "Why is that so?" I persisted. The answer came from the earth, "Many times I have been washed away by floods. Each time, zinc is washed away." The earth added, "Stop putting urea fertilizer here. There is already too much in me." Whatever was said was all recorded on tape.

An agricultural director came from Pune (a major city of India). He said, "Babaji, we want to sow a crop here for research purposes. We will first take a soil sample for testing." I told him, "Use any land you like." The result of their soil test was late in arriving. Before it came, the earth from that field itself told me, "Such and such things are present in me." When the letter arrived describing the results of the soil testing, we compared it with our tape recording of what the earth had said. The results were the same. Our "laboratory" is so powerful that we had stopped our vehicle only for a moment and recorded the whole "test." God's laboratory is so powerful that you may ask about anything anywhere on the earth. I think He will answer as soon as you stop moving your lips to ask.

What is God? God is That which says, "Let it be so!" Whatever you say after taking the name of God will be fulfilled. Even things which are impossible will happen.

Sometimes even the person who speaks God's words does not know what is happening. Recently a couple came who had two daughters but no son. They said to me, "We want a son." I innocently said, "Do volunteer service at the sacred fire (havan) for seven days, wave Chauri Sahib (fly whisk) over Guru Granth

Sahib, and distribute fruit to the congregation. Then you will get a very splendid son. God will say, 'Let it be so!' It is not a big thing for Him."

Then the man told us, "My wife is already pregnant. The doctor has checked and has said, 'The child in her womb is a girl.'" I said to them, "I do not know who spoke. Do this sewa (voluntary service) for seven days. It is not difficult for Him to make a boy from a girl." Yesterday the child was born, and it was a boy. The father was stunned. He said, "The doctors have failed." I told him, "The whole world fails before God."

Where there is dharam, oceans and oceans have coalesced. Scientists will eventually come to the same conclusions that dharmic people have already reached. Science is closely linked to dharam. It is our misfortune that we have not been able to explain dharam at a level that scientists could understand.

The power of the saint is not created by any method of sitting or standing. If one could meet Him by doing postures, you could meet Him by doing any asana you like. Or if you could meet Him through strength, wrestlers would be the first to meet and grasp Him.

What is God? God is Love. It is not that we love God. God loves us.

If your mind is totally focused on your Guru, you see Him in everything. If you are in samadhi (spiritual absorption) and you look at a fan, you will see that your Guru is behind it, moving it with his Light. If you love your Guru, when you look at the ocean and wonder how it is moving, you will see that it is moving by his command. Then you will see God in everything. Saint Nam Dev said, "Everything is God. Everything is God. There is nothing without God." What has happened? As Guru Gobind Singh says, "From two, we have become one." Because of our past karma, there is a wall between us, as thin as a butterfly's wing. When enlightenment comes forth within us, ignorance vanishes, and then we see that everything is God.

When the flame of enlightenment is illumined within you, when you have merged with Him, then you will see only the Light. You will see it in trees, you will see it in water, you will see it in mountains. You will see the Light of God everywhere. This will happen only after meditating, after focusing your mind on your Guru. Once your inner Light is inwardly merged with your Guru's Enlightenment, that Light spreads everywhere.

If anyone asks me, Guru Gobind Singh is not defined by any dress or boundary. Guru Gobind Singh is He Who is the Creator of the cosmos. He is born of it, and he pervades it. Even today he is within everything. How we see God is a matter of a person's faith – God will assume that form.

I have seen only Him

God is very powerful, enlightenment is very powerful, and the saints have spoken extensively about science. But our misfortune is that we get stuck in issues of what to eat, what to wear, how to sit, how to speak, which direction to face when we meditate. The great potential for enlightenment is spoiled by such things. Enlightenment sits to the side, saying, "I have no customers. The people are only concerned with their eating and drinking habits."

Guru Nanak has simply said that any food which provokes evil thoughts is bad, and if some food does not suit your stomach, don't eat it. If by drinking something you feel superior to other human beings or lose control, don't drink it. The Guru has left everything to the individual. He says, "Keep control over your self. Thermometers have been placed in you. Why are you worrying?"

Actually, there is so much potential for enlightenment in a person. Sometimes I think, "If a person wants, with the Grace of God, there is so much power within him that he can change the whole Creation."

One day a woman here asked the volunteer who was irrigating the fields to give water to her fields. He said to her, "You'll get water tomorrow." She quarreled with him, to no avail, and then sent a small boy to me: "Ask Maharaj to send rain." The child came to me, saying, "Babaji, Naniji (grandmother) says, 'Ask Maharaj, 'Let there be rain.''" I said, "It's amazing! So much faith!" I told the child, "Before you return to her with the message, it will rain." I said this with faith. Before he reached her, the rain had begun. I told him to ask her, "Are your fields filled?"

If someone asks me, "What is God?" I will say that the whole Creation is bound under His command. Wherever He points, it moves.

They say that one reaches this stage and that stage in meditation. I have not seen any stages. I have seen only Him. I have not asked Him, "How many stages are there? How many levels of enlightenment are there? What is Your House like?" I say, "If You are there, that is sufficient. You are everything for me."

I have seen only One Thing. I do not speak much about these things. I only say, "Love. He is very merciful. He is forgiving. He is compassionate. He is the Giver of everything. A person who believes in Him will not be disappointed. A person who believes in Him has victory in his grasp, for victory is on his tongue." I have seen that anyone who has faith becomes so lofty in his thinking that no evil remains in him.

Stories from my youth

You speak of healing allergies and such, but these are very minor, ordinary things. When I was so young that I did not have a beard, I wore a sheet around my waist and people used to gather around me at one village. They were fond of drama, and I was immature; not yet accustomed to these spiritual powers. They brought the dead body of a boy and laid it before me. I said, "It is written by the Fifth Guru in Sukhmani Sahib (the psalm of bliss) that if God so wills, He can keep a person alive without breath. Perhaps He may want to do this since they have brought this boy here as if it's a drama." Gyaniji (a devotee who Babaji had blessed with visionary powers) was with me. I asked him to recite Sukhmani Sahib.

When Gyaniji had completed eight verses of *Sukhmani Sahib*, the breath returned to the dead body. When sixteen verses were complete, the dead boy rose and sat up. When all twenty-four verses were finished, the boy cried, "Bole so nihal? Sat Sri Akal!" (We are uplifted when we proclaim, Truth is Eternal!), the traditional Sikh slogan.

From then on life became very difficult for me. Wherever I would walk, people would pick up the soil from beneath my feet. When I used to take a bath, people crowded around, trying to take a handful of my bathwater (for its blessing power). It became very difficult. I thought, "What have I done?"

It is not a big thing to bring a dead body to life, to cure a person's disease, or to heal someone's arm or leg. If we were to write about such instances, there have been hundreds of thousands of such happenings in my life. But I don't want to give much importance to this.

There was a boy who had been blind from birth. He came from Patti village in Amritsar district. Someone told him, "If you go to Babaji, you will be okay when he touches you with his hand." When he entered the boundary of my village, Sarawan Bodla, he told his father, "That is a very big building" (referring to the mosque in Sarawan, which is quite tall). His father wondered, "How does he know?" The boy said, "I can see now." But I don't attach much significance to the fact that God can heal someone's eyes. After all, Who has given these eyes? They are His. Therefore, what can't He do?

Once a woman came who was a very clever journalist. She asked me, "When will I be married?" Immediately the message came from God, "You are a divorcee. The boy you are now seeing is a very rich person. You are afraid to tell him for fear that he may refuse your proposal." She was so surprised that she wrote a big article in her paper, with bold headlines. "I saw a person who was sitting very happily, smiling, like a lion, and full of peace. When anyone passes before him, he reads the person's whole life and continues smiling. Whatever I asked him, the replies were accurate."

The Faces of Peace

(Pammy Studio)

(Ralph Singh)

(Longman Studio)

(Preet)

She was surprised: "What is all this?" I told her, "Don't worry. Meditate. Then you will also be able to see these things. Your inner mirror has become dirty, nothing more. Clean your mirror and it will start shining. You don't need to change the mirror. It just needs to be cleaned a little, nothing more."

Go straight to Him

What is the problem today? Religion has not remained religious. Ignorant people are talking about enlightenment. Irreligious people are talking about religion. Those who do not even dream of being just are talking about justice. Truth has been set aside and individuals have put themselves in its place. When you go deeply into dharam you will know what it is, what yoga is, what postures are, what enlightenment is.

The Fifth Guru spoke from the place where the Great Enlightenment comes from. He had to say, "I have seen that by performing these yogic postures and developing occult powers, people have not gained clear inner vision. They are just confined to the postures – 'Do this asana, do that asana.'" He says, "Your whole attention is focused on your body. When will you reach There? You have to keep your legs like this, your arms like this. Your thoughts are on sitting. When will you get There? You will not achieve anything by confining yourself to these postures. Go straight to Him."

Now the person is sitting tensely, trying to meditate: "Sit like this, look straight, look at this." Oh people, you are looking at these things, but you don't know where He is.

Kabir says, "I do not want a kingdom; I do not want liberation from rebirth. You may say, 'Take this liberation,' or 'Take this kingdom,' but if You are not there, what is liberation to me? I want You. I do not want liberation; I do not want a kingdom. I only want the love of Your lotus feet. You are sitting in every leaf."

Those who have clear vision have understood – "Where You are is not known. You appear as many, then again You become

One." Guru Gobind Singh says, "You have no form, no features, no caste, no class, no lineage. No one can describe Your form, Your colour, Your contour, Your garb. You are eternal, immutable. You are self-illumined, and Your power is limitless." Looking at God in meditation, the Guru says, "Your Light is in the whole world. No one can specify where You live. Your Light is present in every particle." He says to the person, "You are searching to find where He lives, but when you go there, He may not be in that house. Instead, see Him in every leaf."

A person has only one tongue. With one tongue, how can we ever describe the existence of God? The Guru says, "Even if every hair of the body had a tongue, even then we could not describe You."

Nothing affects gyan

When enlightenment arises within, one's attention does not go anywhere else. The person may be sitting among people who are drinking liquor. He himself has also become intoxicated with God's presence. They do not want his intoxication; they are looking at him and laughing. Their intoxication will go away in the morning, but his bliss will never leave, for his entire life. If he is among people who are watching a film, he will say, "Those actors are not in the movie that I have seen." He is sitting in his own world.

What did they do with Mansur (the Sufi saint)? They tore off his skin, cut off his hands, cut off his head. Mansur said, "You have cut off my hands of flesh, but the hands of my gyan are still firmly in their place. You have cut off my head, but the head of my gyan is firmly in place. You have torn off my skin, and you want to annihilate my voice, but even if you destroy my body I will still say, "An al Haqq! (I am the Truth! I am Allah!)" They burnt his body and threw the ashes in the water. The sound, "An al Haqq!" came from the very ashes. When they threw the ashes in the water, "An al Haqq!" came forth from the bubbles. Where the ashes touched a tree, the sound came: "An al Haqq!" The voice said, "Oh my Friend, they want to annihilate my gyan. But my gyan will never end. They are pleased that they have destroyed my body, but wherever the ashes of the body are placed, 'An al Haqq!' will be heard. The water and the tree have become my body, and they are saying, 'An al Haqq! An al Haqq!'"

Such cruel means they have used to try to destroy the saints. One person was sawed in half head first; people were boiled alive. The Fifth Guru was set on a hot iron plate, but still he was still singing God's praises. Gyan is not affected by anything. Water cannot drown it, weapons cannot cut it, nothing can dry it up, nothing can throw light on it. Gyan is gyan.

More stories from the farms

From childhood, I have thought that God is so great that no one can describe Him. We cannot say, "This cannot be done," "That cannot be done," for everything is possible. Set a goal and love God. So much can be done that the person does not know how he is doing it.

I used to stand in the fields the whole day as long as people were working. Once we went to Surajpur (one of Gobind Sadan's early farms). The whole night went by, and the next day, and the next. With a full seventy hours passed while I was standing in the field, and it had no effect on me. I was under the effect of that divine intoxication. I was so happy to see how successfully the work was progressing and how hard the people were working. Because they love me, they thought, "If he is standing here, why shouldn't we work?" So they kept on working. In the morning, I said, "Let's go." Balwant Singh said, "You don't realize it but 70 hours have just passed." Prior to that, I had not known it; I just kept standing.

Once at Shiv Sadan there was a great pile of wheat – thousands of bags – lying in the open after harvesting. My attendant, Gurbux Singh, was sitting next to my cottage. The hukam (divine order) came: "Tell him to take this stick and make a line around that pile of wheat reciting 'Ek Onkar Sat Nam Siri Wahe Guru,'

("There is one God whose name is Truth, Praise the ever more wondrous God"), and sprinkle this water there." I did not know that it would rain cats and dogs that night, but He knew. It rained and rained, but not a single grain of wheat was touched. It rained so hard that there were pools of water standing about, but not a grain was spoiled.

What Name can we call Him? What place is there where He is not?

Sugarcane is subject to red rot, a very serious disease. They say that once it enters a field, it affects the whole area. I was standing next to a field in Shiv Sadan while sugarcane was being planted. As is customary, our volunteers were laying sections cut from the previous year's cane in the furrows. The District Cane Officer arrived, and after him, his senior officer came.

They asked me to stop sowing the crop, saying, "You are sowing a great disease which will spoil the whole area." I told them, "This is the difference between you and me. You senior officers have seen this red rot today. There will be no disease even in this part of the field, let alone the rest of the whole area." When the sugarcane matured, they came back. I asked them to cut a sample of the cane. When they did, they found that there was no disease even in that very place. One officer said, "Babaji, this is something entirely new for us." I told him, "It is new for you because you have no faith in God. For us, the hukam was to take water, touch it with a small sword (kirpan), and sprinkle it on this cane. When that water was sprinkled on the cane, the disease vanished."

Early one morning, I was sitting in meditation, and the Goddess of the River Ganges came and said, "Come to my banks today and drink tea." I called Balwant Singh and asked him to prepare tea for me and the others. He understood, because he was very fond of farming, and he had seen the results of the hukams. Actually, these spiritual Powers are very friendly. Worldly friends may become angry with you sometimes, but the spiritual Powers do not become angry.

It was a very surprising scene. I was sitting there on the banks of the Ganges (which formed the eastern border of Shiv Sadan). At once, Mother Ganges came and said to me, "I have called you for this purpose: I want to give this entire area to you." If you go to that place today you will see that the River Ganges has left the entire area; it shifted its course a mile away from where it was then. When Mata Ganga came to me, She said, "I will shift to that side now, and on this side I will wash away many places." There was a gurdwara in a nearby village on our side of the river. She said, "That gurdwara will be washed away. Tell them." Now you will see a rice crop growing in the riverbed on our side. The wheat crop we sowed there earlier this year produced 240 kilos of wheat per acre. And in that area where She said she would flow, She is now washing away thousands of acres of land. How can I comprehend that water begins talking to me? But these things are recorded.

In reality, if someone asks me, "Where is God?" God is everywhere. Water is under His command. The entire cosmos is under His command. We are also under His command.

You cannot meet Him through methods

Do not let your mind become confined to small things. He can make a poor man a king, and a king a pauper. If He wants, He can say, "Let it be so! You will become a king!" The whole world may be against that person, but he will become a king. In my life, I have seen that He is such a great Power that we cannot describe Him.

I have not gone to any person; I have not read any book. I have talked directly with Him and I ask Him the questions. When you came to me, He, Himself, is giving me instructions. I am just repeating what He said. It is a circle.

You are telling people, "If you do such and such, you will see God." Listen carefully, you will not meet Him with all these methods. The Third Guru wrote, "All the girls went to entertain Him in their own ways. I thought, 'When He looks at them, perhaps

He will look at me also.' So I innocently followed them. They knew how to sing and play musical instruments. I did not know anything; I was not beautiful. I was just standing behind them. But what happened? When He came, I was simple and homely, but He liked me, and He came straight to me. They were all singing their songs, but He was standing by me and asking, 'How are you?' He gave the entire enlightenment to me, while they were busy singing their songs."

Actually, one does not now what will please Him. The Fifth Guru says, "I have no method or sweet song for attracting the Master. I said, 'Please accept my innocence and bless me.' He blessed me so much and looked at me so mercifully that He took me to God." He is unique. You cannot meet Him through any methods.

The dervishes used to travel by flying; they had such spiritual powers. Guru Nanak used to close his eyes and carry his two companions along with him, and thus they would reach their destination. But Guru Nanak says this is not a matter of any yogic posture. It is a matter of love alone. Where can He not carry you? He can show you the entire Creation.

They tell me you are a great scientist and have met many great people. By meeting good people you will gain knowledge. But don't become so immersed in your books that you do not know where He is. A book is for reading. A book will not carry you to Him.

Saint Ravidas said to God, "I was bound by my ignorance, and now I have bound You in the bondage of love. By meditating upon You, I have been freed from ignorance. Now try to free Yourself from my love." God replied, "Before love, I have no recourse."

God can be seen everywhere

God is everywhere, the Giver of Light, of Enlightenment, of Love, He pervades everything. Guru Gobind Singh saw God in everything. He was an enlightened being, and he was also a hero, for the times were such that he had to defend the people. Women were being abducted and the people were being oppressed by tyrannical rulers. He said to God, "You are the arrow, You are the shield, You are the spear, You are the sword. You are the cry of victory, and You are the Hero of the World. Sometimes when I unsheathe my sword, even the sun is frightened before its glory. Your glory is so great that it cuts out hordes of fools and casts them aside."

Guru Gobind Singh said, "I have not come to tell people to close their eyes and be hypocrites. I have come to rise above hypocrisy. I have not come to pitch a tent as an obstacle on the road where people have to pass. I will repeat whatever He has said to me: I will not remain silent in this ephemeral world. I have come to awaken courage in the people. I have no enmity against anyone. I have come to make everyone victorious."

In his enlightenment, Guru Gobind Singh saw God everywhere. He used to see God even in his horse: When the horse ran, he said, "It is You who are racing." He said, "You're the Dancer of the Dance. You are setting the whole world dancing, and You are looking at the spectacle. You are the spear, You are the arrow, You are the shield. When they are in my hands and You are with me, there will be victory, for I have taken up arms to protect the weak."

Guru Gobind Singh explained heroism, as well as meditation and enlightenment. He also taught very high moral character. He said to men, "You should not violate the honour of another man's wife even in your dreams, and your love for your own wife should increase every day. All day you meet people; keep your gaze pure. Consider women of your own age your sisters, younger women your daughters, and older women your mothers."

If anyone has faith in God, his mind will never waver. The whole world may be against him, but He is the pinnacle of courage. In military service, one learns what faith is. There was one Brigadier Randhawa (a great devotee of Babaji). A battle was going on in Mizoram (an Indian border state). Brigadier Randhawa was sitting in his vehicle as his forces were being fired upon. See how God saves His devotees: As if by chance, Brigadier Randhawa stepped out of the vehicle. Within one minute, the vehicle was hit. What happened? God had told him, "Get aside." Then he immediately got back into the same vehicle. Why? Because he had faith, and also innocence. He said, "God is already with us, standing by our side." Another person may say, "God, God," as much as he wants, but there is nothing in it. If he passes a snake, he will run away in fear. If anyone merely threatens him, he will run away. Faith gives inner courage. The Ninth Guru gave this instruction: "Neither intimidate nor be intimidated by anyone."

Therefore, my feeling is, What is God? God is Grace, Heroism, Love, Willpower, and continuous Blessing. There are great stores of everything in God. What lessons we take from them? That is for us to consider.

Planetary Difficulties

If the demons had not usurped the kingdom of the gods, then the goddess Durga would not be worshipped today. She appeared only because she heard the cries of the kind-hearted people. Perhaps if there had not been murderous conditions in Arabia, the Prophet Muhammad might not have appeared. Perhaps if there had not been intolerance, abductions, and looting in India, Guru Nanak would not have appeared. At such times, good trees sprout which yield good fruit forever. Throughout history, when did the great good people come? When many people were bad.

Obstacles bring forth truth. When obstacles occur, know that God will come. When the path is clear, know that God will not come. He will just be sitting in a relaxed mood. He is so great, with so many powers, but He is usually silent. His Power will come only to remove obstacles. If there is no obstacle troubling you, why need He come? But when we are surrounded by difficulties, He stands between us and the obstacles, strikes with His two-edged sword, and commands, "Be gone!" Then there is rejoicing.

People are afraid when dark clouds gather and thunder clashes. But clouds and thunder are nothing; they are only the sources of rain for the hot and parched earth. Do not be afraid of clouds; do not be afraid of difficulties. Keep moving straight ahead. Give your hand to God, and He will keep you in the light twenty-four hours a day. Dharam can never be defeated. Dharam is victorious day and night. If you leave dharam, you will always be defeated.

As it is said in Gurbani, the world is on fire. But "The way of the devotee is different from the way of the world. The path the devotee treads is sharper than the edge of a sword and finer than a hair." To stay on this straight path, get up early in the morning; meditate; do havan make the aura of your mind very strong; remain happy.

Always read Jaap Sahib (Guru Gobind Singh's empowering cosmic hymn in praise of God); it will give you tremendous power. God has given us a huge boon in Jaap Sahib. The vision was given to us at Gobind Sadan that wherever Jaap Sahib is placed, read, and respected, nothing bad will happen. Even bombs will have no effect there. If you read Jaap Sahib, you will be surrounded by a fortress of light.

For these times, meditate so that the religious qualities within you will develop: righteousness, justice, love, truth, understanding others' problems as your own. And do not worry. There is no need for worry, because this period will not last; another period will come. There is only need for the grace of God.

Natural Disasters

After the devastating earthquake in Gujarat, India in 2001

Everything is under God's control – darkness as well as light, conflict as well as peace. The heavens, lower worlds, planets, oceans, winds and water all go by His order. If the natural world is not under God's control, then all the prophets and scriptures are wrong. Events like this are not within the control of any human. This earthquake occurred according to the order of God. We cannot criticize God's order. God is unerring.

Perhaps the places where the victims will take their next births are already decided. This is God's programme. In India we believe in rebirth and in karma – the consequences of our thoughts and actions.

A natural creation of God has erupted. We can only pray, "Oh God, we human beings are Your family. You are like a farmer who harvests his crop whether it be unripe, ripe, or half-ripe. This was Your crop, which You Yourself were caring for. Someone's child, someone's father and mother have gone, someone has gone at half his full age."

God knows what He has done. We can only pray, "We cannot bear such dreadful wrath, but we cannot object as to why it has been done. You have created us. We are Your garden. You are to look after us. We cannot interfere in where You will plant Your seedlings. You are our Owner."

We cannot challenge God's order, but we can worship, recite scripture, conduct havan, and request through such worship, "We people are too weak to tolerate such disasters. Please bless those souls who have passed on, so that they shall not wander and may have a good new life. Please meet the needs of those who are living. By Your great mercy, may such a tragedy not occur again. If there are to be earthquakes, please send them to uninhabited wildernesses."

It is one thing to give material to help to those who are suffering, but the greatest thing is to beg for God's mercy. God can end all difficulties. In our time, many people have abandoned worship of God. As it is written in the Guru Granth Sahib, "God is hungry for love and devotion."

In Gobind Sadan, Jaap Sahib, Chandi Di War, and Hanuman Chalisa are being recited around the clock so that humanity may enjoy peace and prosperity. I appeal to the whole world to worship and read scriptures, requesting God that such a disaster may not occur in any country in the future. The devotional activities in Gobind Sadan are meant to bring peace and pleasure in the world, to end crime, and to bring love among people. It is our prayer that no thorn should prick anyone.

There can never be any danger to that inner light. It is all Love. God wants us to love each other, to help each other, to stand together in sorrow and in happiness. We all have one Father and we are all His family, no matter whether we follow Islam, or Christianity, or Hinduism, or Sikhism. His messengers keep coming to us so that we will know that He exists, whether we call Him Allah, Paramatma, Ram, or the Great Power. God is so merciful, so powerful that we should all remain happy, but we are not. We are always worried, for we have no faith in God. We should obey His orders and love Him. We should turn within and meditate in order to, as Buddha taught, purge our inner evils and bar evils from entering from outside. Then, as it is written in the Guru Granth Sahib, "You are me and I am You. There is no difference between understand. But when we turn within we begin to perceive God us." The same thing is written in the Vedas, "What You are, I am." God is "neti, neti" – "beyond, beyond," beyond our ability to see or pervading everywhere, doing everything.

Goodness Will Spread

To Anatoli Kim, a famous writer from Kazakhstan

Anatoli began with the question: Which will ultimately win—darkness or light?

Babaji answered: I am speaking from that Power which is only One, and whatever I say you will see with your own eyes. It will spread throughout the world but it will take time. Slowly goodness will come to everyone, for good people everywhere. When bad people come to power, hatred spreads among the people. Then they have to become good. When the supply finishes, the shop will close. Right now there is still plenty of hatred to run their shops. Now there is conflict because conflict is being supplied. When the sun rises, it gives light to everyone. Its rays reach even those who don't want it. When truth comes, it will spread throughout the world.

Question: You speak of truth. Is it the same for everyone?

Babaji: Truth means it is the same for everyone. Where there are boundaries, there is no truth. Your country and its buildings are beautiful, but people have moved away from truth. When truth dawns, that beauty will emerge again. Your ideas will surely influence people. There are no boundaries around truth or around ideas. It is only a concept that Russia and India are separate. In truth, there is only One.

Question: Do you think there is more power with good or evil?

Babaji: Goodness is very powerful. It will uproot evil. The battle between good and evil will continue, but truth will be victorious. Right now there is darkness.

Question: How will we know that truth is coming?

Babaji: It will rise before your eyes. It will start as an inner feeling, and then spread throughout the world. A philosopher is very firm in his thoughts. You need a very strong crane to move him. By that I mean that only one with truth and great ideas can change his mind. Only that person asks me questions who really wants to learn. We are both students. When you ask me, I ask from There, and we both receive enlightenment. There is no effort required; it is all His choice. It is just a matter of love. It is from the place of Love.

The World Will Not End

Message to a Russian group expecting a disastrous apocalypse at the turn of the millennium

It is true that the planets and stars have a strong influence on earthly events. India's ancient seers and astrologers have described these effects in great detail in their books. From the beginning, rays have been traveling throughout the cosmos, planets have been created and destroyed, earthquakes and floods have occurred, some species have become extinct and others have appeared, civilizations rise and fall. Good and bad things are continually occurring. Whatever will happen, will happen. But the world will not come to an end. Let God deal with His own domain. You should just love God. God Himself will change things or provide safeguards, for we are all His family.

God creates diseases, and also medicines to cure the diseases. God creates destructive rays and also repairing rays. People are afraid of death, but they cannot see that a person who dies from cancer is freed, and that he is greeted with great rejoicing wherever he is reborn as a baby in his next life. Destructive effects do form in the cosmos, but other forces are also created and come together to counteract them. You have seen only one event, but perhaps you have not seen many other cosmic processes which would save the world from what you have seen.

We have a story in Punjabi: There was a bird which nests on the ground and sleeps with its legs in the air. Someone asked the bird, "Why do you sleep with your legs towards the sky?" She answered, "If I lower my legs, the sky will fall down." She was told, "The sky is not going to fall. You can sleep in peace."

After the great flood covered the earth, God made a commitment that He would never again destroy life on this planet. God said to Noah, "As long as earth lasts, sowing and reaping, cold and heat, summer and winter, day and night shall cease no more." (Genesis 9). God never goes back on His commitment.

There are always great dramas going on in the cosmos. Many things come into existence which cannot be seen with the naked eye. They are so numerous that they cannot be counted. Some come into existence very briefly and then die. If we are looking through a telescope, some things may not yet have come into existence, but may do so just after we stop looking through the lens. What we saw may have been destructive, but what we did not see was something which came afterwards, which might have a positive effect. Both forces may unite and the harmful effect will end. Things that we cannot see keep developing and dying out on their own, again and again.

There are certain tiny forms of matter which do not even last for one second, but they leave an impact. When their effect acts upon certain destructive elements, it turns them into something very good. The cosmos is an elaborate show in which nothing is as it appears to be. Just by seeing one aspect of it, you cannot understand the rest.

For example, in one vision you may see certain worlds that seem about to be destroyed by cosmic events. But those events may appear to happen in that particular moment only. But if you keep watching, the very forces which you thought would be destructive instead form a barrier, and this barrier breaks the speed of other destructive whirlwinds. If you focused on them at one time only, you would have predicted that those worlds would be annihilated. But the other waves may have a different effect later.

Sometimes you may see what looks like a bombardment of particles that make holes in a planet's atmosphere. But if you look again a little later, you may see that the holes have been repaired. This is the way the cosmic show goes on. A person who sees the holes will predict that there will be a great heat wave because heat will pour through the holes unobstructed. But later those holes close because new rays come in. I've seen layers that I can only describe as similar to layers of rust on iron that appear they will destroy the worlds below. But then other layers start moving in, and those rust-like layers are destroyed.

There are innumerable galaxies, not just this one in which we are living. I have seen that there are other worlds which are very, very big – much bigger than our planet. And there is something like a great pit in the cosmos which is so big that millions of earths like ours would fit into it.

There is a tremendous spectacle going on above. You have become frightened by just a tiny part of that drama. There is so much more to be seen.

Is There Any Hope?

To a national television broadcaster

Now everything in the world has been turned upside down, and only God can put it right. But it will be all right. All the prophets have promised that when times are very hard, peace will certainly follow. One cannot live forever under pressure. Change will come, and good people will come forward.

Now people are following bad examples. When someone imitates a bad person, how can he become good? When you see a successful person, always ask yourself how he or she has succeeded. If it through honesty, good character, truthful speech, and just actions, then you must watch and follow their examples.

But if a person has become successful by grabbing what does not belong to him, never go near him, for he will always speak of falsehood.

Whenever goodness is suppressed, the Power of God starts bringing Light. What is going on now is a mere show, and it will not last for long. It is all temporary, with no foundation. It exists only in the air, with no footing on the ground.

In all ages both goodness and evil have existed. Guru Nanak says that this Kali Yuga is actually a good time to live, because if you have faith in God, you will quickly become enlightened. Why? Because in such times those who call to God are very few.

Guru Gobind Singh wrote in strict terms that such negative events beyond anyone's imagination would come to pass. One hundred percent of what he predicted is indeed now happening. Guru Nanak wrote that Kali Yuga is a chariot of fire, and falsehood is the horse pulling it.

However, there is an eternal rule that as a person commits bad deeds, his power diminishes. Similarly, because this time in history has witnessed so much evil, the power and also the length of this period will decrease. There is nothing to be discouraged about. It is a very dangerous period, but it is of limited duration, and everything will change.

Postscript

Maharaj ji's Message

12-23-07

Maharaj ji lay quietly on his bed. Meanwhile, the world of His faithful prayed and expected that even now He would get up. After all, He had healed them of the incurable, solved their intractable personal and business problems, subdued terrorist outbreaks, brought bounty forth from wastelands, and blessed them with a life lasting peace to their troubled minds. There was nothing He couldn't do, even conquer death, if He willed it. As I tuned my mind to His words, He spoke clearly and sharply:

> **"I have nothing to prove. You may want to see a miracle for your faith. But I need nothing. I have lived my faith. Any questions, the record stands and speaks for itself. If you want a miracle, you do it. I have done mine. I have transformed all of you into Warriors for Truth. I've made heroes out of cowards, and the story has not even begun. You will see such Light and happenings that you could never have believed. As I have said, again, and again I will work even greater deeds through you. All will join you in this mission. Do not despair. I am always with you to bring joy. Let there be no sadness. The pain of separation is for those attached to a body. My spirit always has been and always will be with all of you. Recite Nam. Do Jaap Sahib. Love each other, and welcome all who come in my name."**

Early the next morning, He had left. In passing as in life, Maharaj ji's connection with Jesus will be etched in history. He left on Christmas eve, was cremated on Christmas, and His memorial was held on the Day of Epiphany, January 6th, Orthodox Christmas.

When people ask: "How did He die?" I say, "He didn't. Great souls take our sins on themselves and leave when it is their time." "How old was He?" I respond, "Ageless. He has been with us forever and will remain for eternity." We may ask one thousand "whys" but as Maharaj ji Himself stated, "I have nothing else to prove. I have lived my faith." Now let us live ours.

Ralph Singh

Editor's notes

Most of these talks were addressed in response to a question. That may have either been posed by an individual directly, a world issue that Babaji wanted to address, or that Babaji sensed was at the heart of an individual's dilemma. Some were written out and delivered to a particular group on Babaji's behalf as indicated by "Message in the the title," seldom attended the hundreds of gatherings to which he was invited.

He used to say he was too busy working to solve the problems to take time and important funds just to address a large audience.

His talks were always spontaneous. There was never any preparation. Yes, we may say that in large gatherings Babaji may have given some forethought to the matter. He's been concerned about major issues in the world all his life and most probably for all his past lives as well.

While we, who had the luxury and privilege of sitting at his feet, and those who have had the joy of actually translating his discourses, can tell you that he himself knew everything, he would never take credit for any act or any statement.

He would always say, "Ask me any question. When you do, the Voice inside me answers and I learn, too."

And when what can only be termed miracles would spring from lips it was as if God was answering his every thought. Babaji would correct us, that it was in fact God's will that this was happening and he was only the vehicle.

But we have witnessed and according to Babaji will continue to witness proof that God sits on the tongue of His saints. That whatever they say or even think does come true.

This is the authentic process through which that which is not visible to the ordinary individual suddenly becomes so apparent that it is impossible to miss; unless, of course, you turn away. But as Babaji has promised in this time to come, there will be no turning away. The Light of God from which and through which all joy, goodness, Truth, and justice emerges will literally surround us and there will be no chance for denial. As Babaji has said, when the Light appears, the darkness literally vanishes and as we become accustomed to the Light we will wonder how the darkness ever existed.

So enjoy these talks and let their arrows penetrate your minds and hearts that the Light of God's love fills you all.

If there is any confusion after reading these, it is solely due to the poor job of the editors and is no reflection of Babaji or his words.

A brief note about translation

Punjabi as a language is the language of "rulers" where the imperative is the norm, and the force of the individual "I" is standard. Babaji, though very much a product and advocate of that culture, chose to use "we" and the passive voice, in his discourses to indicate that he was fully conscious that it was God speaking through him rather than him speaking his own mind. And yet the experience of being in his physical presence was so powerful, that we have taken the liberty of using an active voice in our translations to fully express it.

Our thanks to our Editorial team of Mary Pat Fisher, NarSingh Dev, Virginia Satterfield, Alan Nykamp, Joginder Kaur, and many others for their help in preparing and compiling these documents, and to the Kandhari family for their generous support.

Ralph Singh

Director, Publications and Public Relations

Glossary

amrit – nectar; the baptismal drink of Khalsa made in iron implements mixing water and sugar wafers with the double edged sword, while each of five Khalsa recite the five daily prayers respectively; originally administered by Guru Gobind Singh

asana – yogic postures

atma – soul

avtars – incarnations of God

Bhawani – one name for the Goddess

chakra – vortex in the body

Chauri Sahib – fly whisk; waved reverently over Guru Granth Sahib or other objects of veneration

dervish – Muslim term for saint

Dharam – (Dharma) God's eternal order, from the laws of nature which hold everything from the cosmos to the sub-atomic particles in balance; applied to human life it refers to spirituality; the universal teachings of God which empower a person to maintain a righteous life and bring justice to the world

Durga Mata – the Goddess; Parvati, Lord Shiv ji's wife; usually seen riding on her tiger

Ek Onkar Sat Nam Siri Wahe Guru – There is one God whose name is Truth. Praise the ever more wondrous, ever greater God; Nam given by Baba Virsa Singh ji

Gurbani – the Guru's teachings, typically as enshrined in Guru Granth Sahib

Guru Granth Sahib – Holy scripture of the Sikhs, revered as the Eternal Guru

gyan – enlightenment; inner wisdom; enlightened wisdom

hukam – divine order, as transmitted through God's messengers; refers to daily readings from Guru Granth Sahib

Jap ji Sahib – Guru Nanak's preamble to Guru Granth Sahib and first daily prayer of a Sikh

Ka'aba (Ka'bah) – Holiest sanctuary of Islam in Mecca, part of which was built by Abraham and Ismael, which contains the sacred black stone.

kafir – unbeliever; one who suppresses the truth

Kali Yuga – the present age; considered the darkest, most corrupt of times

karah prasad – blessed offering distributed to everyone regardless of race or creed in every Gurdwara; a sweet pudding made of sugar, ghee, and flour; a food for the gods that Guru Nanak brought back from Heaven

karma – fruit of our actions, whether in this life or in the past; literally actions

kharbs of yojans – the ancient measurement by which the distance between planets and other heavenly bodies was described (1 kharb yojan = 250,000,000,000,000 miles)

khir – rice pudding

kirat – Guru Nanak's spiritual path of working hard to support yourself and sharing the fruits of your labor with others

kirpan – sword; one of the five symbols of Khalsa; mostly worn today as a small ceremonial sword

lakh – one hundred thousand

mu'min – in Islam, a believer; one who stands for truth

Nam – God's Holy Name; the name of God;

> Ek Onkar Sat Nam Siri Wahe Guru – There is one God whose name is Truth. Praise the Ever more wondrous God; Nam given by Baba Virsa Singh ji

Nami – God; the One who is named

Naniji – grandmother

nawab – local ruler

neti – infinite; that which is beyond

Panj Piaras – Five Beloveds; first five members of Khalsa that Guru Gobind Singh personally baptized

Paramatma – God; literally, Supreme soul; Emerson's "oversoul"

pir – Muslim saint

puja – the term for prayer and worship in Hindu tradition; form of prayer and worship

Rabia – the great eighth-century female Muslim saint of Iraq

ragi – one who sings the Guru's hymns; integral part of Sikh worship

samadhi – spiritual absorption

sangat – congregation

sewa – voluntary service

sewadar – devotees who serve the community

Sahibzadas – the four sons of Guru Gobind Singh who were martyred: the older two in battle and the younger two, by burying them alive in a wall

shabd – God's Holy Name; literally, word

shabds – Names of God; alternatively, hymns sung from Gurbani

Sukhmani Sahib – the psalm of bliss; Guru Arjan Dev ji's hymn of peace in Guru Granth Sahib

surat – attention; consciousness

The Sikh Gurus – the spiritual Light Guru Nanak Dev ji (1469 - 1539) passed to nine successors. Guru Gobind Singh ji (1666 – 1708) the tenth Guru, then coronated Guru Granth Sahib, "Eternal Guru" in 1708.

The tenth door – the portal to the spiritual realm; nine portals to the material world are visible, i.e. eyes, ears, nose, mouth, etc;

Tirthankaras – incarnations or prophets within the Jain tradition

Vedas – ancient scriptures of India

References for the talks

The talks in bold have been published in *Gobind Sadan Times*, our newsletter. The dates of the talks closely correspond to the date of publication, but do not match exactly.

"A TURBAN FOR PEACE"

"Those Who Love God Must Care for the Needs of All Humanity"
Baba Virsa Singh touched and healed people at all levels of society and personally demonstrated how to solve the most intractable problems that plague the world. Here are some testimonials to his work.

Impact on India
"What impresses me most is that Babaji has offered us a practical example of how we as a nation and a world can overcome our religious differences by respecting all religions. Babaji himself worked and linked people to the land and showed the way for our country to progress."

Kuldip Nayar, eminent journalist and fmr. Rajya Sabha member,
Fmr. High Commissioner to England

"Serving humanity is a great work. What Babaji teaches is very important at the present juncture, as we are passing through a critical time in the country as well as the world. We have to develop a feeling of kindness, and after meeting Babaji we have to improve. The glory on his face is tremendous. One who looks at him thinks that all his problems are either going to be minimized or solved. God has blessed him and he is a blessing for all those searching for peace."

Sri Motilal Vora, Treasurer, India National Congress Party,
Fmr. Governor, U.P. (India's largest state)

"If we want to strengthen the fabric of Indian society, then we should all adopt the teachings of Baba Virsa Singh. Babaji has had a great role in uniting our nation. If the leadership of India would listen to Baba Virsa Singh then we would not have any problems."

Sri Ashok Singhal, Int'l Chairman, Vishwa Hindu Parishad

Impact on Russia

"The world needs spiritual directions, which we have found at Gobind Sadan. Here we find what is missing in Russia in our grey everyday life. No doubt, we must get rid of poverty. Poverty is not an isolated problem. If we solve the problems from a spiritual perspective and transform human consciousness, then we will receive the wisdom to solve all our problems. The teachings of Baba Virsa Singh are the real mechanism of transformation"

Yuriy Ageshin, Pro-rector Russian School of Private Law and Legal advisor to the Duma

"In 2004 Babaji together with his delegation were in Russia and met with deputies of the State Duma, with Luzhkov, the mayor of Moscow, and I am sure that the fact of the better and faster development of economy in Russia, happened due to Babaji as well. Because Babaji helped so many people who met him for the first time to rethink the way we are living today and point us in the right direction."

Svetlana Smirnova, Deputy, State Duma and Member PACE

Overcoming Religious Conflict

"Baba Virsa Singh reminds us of and indeed belongs to the chain of the great saints and sages of India who have brought the people together through their extraordinary powers, which include the power of love. We should learn from him the vital lesson of loving and helping not only people within a particular religious community but all those outside it and establish the religion of humanity which is the cornerstone of all great religions and the only road to survival."

Dr. S. A. Ali, Founder member of Hamdard University:

"I want to say that I deeply appreciate and admire Babaji as the presence of God to me. The light that comes from him washes away all my darkness. We must thank God that someone like Babaji is living in our midst. The presence of one holy soul is a great blessing to the world."

The Late Father Paulos Mar Gregorios, Fmr Metropolitan, Past-President World Council of Churches

"Whatever theological interpretation one may give to the role and message of Baba Virsa Singh and to what is happening under his inspiration at Gobind Sadan, one cannot deny the power of this man's example and message: he and his community show us how persons of all religions can transcend their differences and come together to work for the poor and the transformation of this world."

Paul F Knitter, Paul Tillich Professor of Theology, World Religions and Culture at Union Theological Seminary in the City of New York.

Overcoming Poverty

"In my international development career, when working with the poor to help them get out of poverty I have always started with what they had rather with what they needed. It is a self- empowerment approach. The work is worship approach pioneered by Babaji at Gobind Sadan is the spiritual soul mate of my work. My transition to this type of thinking was certainly though subtly influenced through my first encounter with Babaji 14 years ago."

Dr. Naresh Singh, fmr Exec. Director, UNDP Commission, Legal Empowerment of the Poor

Overcoming Terrorism

"Unlike today, this was a period of relative calm in India and the term 'terrorism' was virtually unheard of. So the violence in Mizoram, especially the triple assassination was a real shock. Baba Virsa Singh ji's role in providing vision and counsel, through I.G. Gurnam Singh Randhawa and the guidance he gave me personally can not be overstated. His spiritual presence was indeed the determining factor in bringing peace. But the lessons we have learned and model we have gained are definitely transferable."

S.K. Chhibber, Former Governor, Indian State of Mizoram

Inspiring the Ideals of Khalsa and the legacy of Guru Nanak

"For over 40 years, Babaji has been working very quietly behind the scenes in order to remove the conflicts that are taking place among religions, among families, within villages, and between political and religious groups. Babaji's aim in life is to teach people to think of peace and not of conflict. This is message is badly needed today. In the way that a pious soul, God's messenger does it, Babaji has been teaching us who live in one world but in so many different ways how to live as one nation and as one human family."

Late Dr. Bhai Mohan Singh – fmr. Chair,
Gobind Sadan Society for Interfaith Understanding

"Even though Babaji himself had never been to school, he was able to answer even my most difficult questions. Babaji's personal example of honest hard work and loving God, set the model of Khalsa for me throughout my life."

Ranjit Singh Kalha, Member, Human Rights Commission,
Fmr Foreign Secretary, Gov't of India

"What Babaji has accomplished in teaching meditation and bringing everyone together to demonstrate the equality of humanity, and bringing all religions together in one place in Gobind Sadan is a great work. Now he is focusing the world, especially India and Russia on the scourge of poverty. This is such an enormous contribution to the legacy of Guru Nanak. He has given practical shape to his teachings, and demonstrated how to work hard, thank God, and share with those in need."

Tarlochan Singh, MP and fmr. Chair, National Commission for Minorities

For more information, contact Ralph Singh,
Director of Publications and Public Relations
Ralph@gobindsadan.org,9818255713,U.S.315-440-1242 or
Mary 2680-1653, marypfisher@hotmail.com
His Holiness Baba Virsa Singh ji Maharaj Memorial Trust
Dr. Rai Singh, 9311010013, Chairman, Harvinder Singh, 9311020013, Secretary
Gadaipur, Mehrauli, New Delhi 110030 INDIA
011-91-11-26801653, 91-11-268022251, FAX 91-11-2680-3398
www.gobindsadan.org Gobindsadan-rus.info;
info@gobindsadan.org